Dreams in the Spirit

Following Your Dreams Toward Your God-Given Destiny

Volume One

Dreams in the Spirit

Following Your Dreams
Toward Your God-Given Destiny

Volume
One

Bart Druckenmiller

Take note that the name satan and related names are not capitalized. We choose not to acknowledge him, even to the point of violating grammatical rules.

Treasure House

An Imprint of

Destiny Image® Publishers, Inc.
P.O. Box 310
Shippensburg, PA 17257-0310

"For where your treasure is,
there will your heart be also." Matthew 6:21

ISBN 1-56043-346-9

For Worldwide Distribution
Printed in the U.S.A.

Dedication

To my beloved children, Daniel, Karis, and Joshua, that they may fulfill their dreams!

Thus speaketh the Lord God of Israel, saying, Write thee all the words that I have spoken unto thee in a book (Jeremiah 30:2).

I will stand upon my watch, and set me upon the tower, and will watch to see what He will say unto me, and what I shall answer when I am reproved. And the Lord answered me, and said, ***Write the vision****, and make it plain upon tables, that he may run that readeth it. For the vision is yet for an appointed time, but at the end it shall speak, and not lie: though it tarry, wait for it; because it will surely come, it will not tarry* (Habakkuk 2:1-3).

Acknowledgments

There are many people I want to thank, for without them you would not be holding this book.

Most of all, I want to thank the Holy Spirit. He is the One to whom I owe all the credit. Never would one page have been written without Him.

Next, I want to thank my wonderful wife, Sue. She is not only my partner and the love of my life, but she is also my best friend. She helped me with the typing and much of the editing. Without her help, I doubt this book would have come to birth.

Special thanks also go to Ankur for his computer expertise. Thank you, Ankur, for all the times you responded to our desperate calls when our Microsoft Word was acting up on us.

I also want to thank Russ and Beverly Kruse for their counsel and wisdom; Bansi, Sarla, Ankur, and Rachana Brahmbhatt for their love and friendship; and Deborah

Peppers and the staff at KJSL for all their support. I also want to thank my family and friends and the people at Life Christian Center for believing in me even though some of the things I was experiencing seemed a little unusual at first.

Sue and I would like to acknowledge our pastors, Rick and Donna Shelton, Virgil and Bonnie Sprock, and Mike and Penny Shepherd, who have encouraged us more than they probably know.

Also special thanks go to Don Nori, Jr., Jeff Hall, and the staff at Destiny Image and Treasure House for believing in and with us to help make this dream a reality. I also want to thank all the men and women of faith whose writings, words, and examples have stirred my heart to believe in my dreams.

We would also like to acknowledge those who journeyed with us to India: Butch Hickerson, Jane Reichard, Sheila Brase, John Reichardt, Kathy and Aaron Senter, Derek Davidson, and Henry Harvey, as well as all our intercessors. Also special thanks go to Roy and Melanie Davidson, who led us and our team and were faithful to the Lord in fulfilling His purpose.

We want to dedicate this book to all those who love our Lord Jesus Christ. Our prayer is that those who read this book will experience God's unfailing love for them and that the Lord will use this book as a springboard in the lives of many to encourage them to follow their dreams toward their God-given destiny.

Endorsement

Today, very few know or understand anything about the connection or relationship that dreams and visions have with destiny. Bart, a dear friend of mine, has summed up by the Spirit of God, the dreams that he and some others have had in the Body of Christ. This book will encourage this generation on the importance of dreams, which are divinely inspired and given by God concerning your personal destiny.

Dreams and visions are windows to the supernatural. By them, God allows you to see beyond the natural into the realms of glory, where Heaven's decisions about your personal life, destiny, and ministry are made.

It is such a privilege and an honor to promote such a book that is so needed today, which is written by a man of God who has experienced the manifestation of this subject.

In this book, Bart teaches by the Spirit of the Lord how to hold onto and fulfill the dreams and visions God gives you...plus much more! Hang on as you enjoy this God-inspired, treasured edition, written for you in this last time!

David E. Taylor
Resurrection Media Ministries

Contents

Foreword

Reading this book took me back to the early days of my Christian life. I believe we all desire a closer walk with our Lord and want to hear Him speak to us. One way He does this is through dreams and visions. Now, after 30 years of this walk with my dear Friend, Savior, and beloved Jesus, I am delighted to be part of this book by writing these few lines.

When I first met Bart and Sue, I fell in Christian love with these two. I praise God for bringing them my way and I believe with all my heart that God Almighty has brought us together for a purpose. My prayer is that God's purpose will be fulfilled and that every word written in this book will be used to revive His Church and bring the lost to His throne of grace. I pray that this book will be used to help reveal to all readers God's love, purposes, and plans for them.

This labor of love will be worth it all if those who read these pages will let the Holy Spirit speak to their hearts.

Bansi Brahmbhatt
International pastor, and founder of Friends of Asia

Preface

Many years ago, I received two very vivid and clear dreams. These are what make up Chapters One and Two. At the time I received them, I knew nothing about the particular subject I am writing about. I was not raised in a church or ministry that promoted such revelations of the Spirit, and I didn't have the faintest idea that the Lord worked in such a manner. Recently, though, I have learned otherwise. In the past few years, I have experienced what some might call prophetic dreams and visions. I believe that these were given not only for me, but to be shared with anyone who desires a closer walk with the Lord.

I was very abruptly introduced to the subject of dreams and visions on the night of May 15, 1995. After having just read the first four chapters in a book called *The Harvest,* written by Rick Joyner of Morning Star Ministries, I became deeply convicted of my shallow walk with the Lord. I felt a great need to spend time in prayer seeking Him.

After a short time of sitting up in bed praying in the spirit, the Spirit of the Lord spoke to me. With my own ears I actually heard ten words being spoken. This came as a complete shock to me. In one night, the Holy Spirit not only spoke to me but also gave me an open vision while I was still awake in my bed.

I don't share this to make myself out as someone whom I am not. I know what a mess I am at times, and I am very aware of my human imperfections. Why God chose to speak to me in this manner is beyond me, I assure you. Nevertheless, because I want to be found faithful, I share what He has given me with the hope that many will start to seek the Lord with all their heart and will begin to discover His plan for their lives. In Chapter Ten, I share in detail these ten words and the vision I was given at that time.

Some of the experiences and dreams I have received have been given for my own wisdom and knowledge. Others have been for my church or for different people I've been associated with. Still others, I believe, have been given for the Body of Christ as a whole. This is not some experience or gift I sought after or asked for, but one that has been a tremendous blessing in my life.

Throughout much of this writing, I know that I will be speaking to people who believe that God works in this manner and who may have had similar experiences. However, I also know that many will pick up this book who have never experienced these things. These people may read it out of curiosity, controversy, or even doubt. Regardless of the motivation of the reader, my prayer is that these revelations will be a blessing to all who read them.

I pray that this book will cause those who don't yet know the Lord or who have never truly had an encounter with

Christ to get to know Him as the wonderful Savior and Lord that He is. For those who have already received Him, my prayer is that the information and anointing on this book will help them have an even closer walk with Him.

I also want to say that just because I have experienced these things doesn't mean in any way that I think I am more spiritual than others or that I have a special gift that others do not have. The Lord can speak to anyone by this means. As He says clearly in Acts 2:17, He will do just that as the days draw nearer to Christ's return:

> *And it shall come to pass in the last days, saith God, I will pour out of My Spirit upon all flesh: and your sons and your daughters shall prophesy, and your young men shall see visions, and your old men shall dream dreams.*

Both men and women in the Body of Christ whom I have spoken with have been experiencing many more dreams and visions recently than in most of their Christian lives. This increase indicates a prophetic picture that we truly are nearer to our blessed hope when we will behold Christ in all His glory. I've written this book to help clarify the purpose and meaning of dreams and visions, and to show how, despite my own shortcomings, these things can be used for God's purposes.

While I was in the process of writing this book, John Reichardt, a good friend of mine who journeyed with our group to India, came up to me at church and asked if I was writing a book. He told me that he was given a dream in which he saw me with pen and paper in hand busily writing something. This was quite an encouragement to me. When we know that God is for us and is thinking about us daily, then with His help, we can do almost anything (see Ps. 139:1-4; Rom. 8:31).

I believe that this book, like many others, has come about because of a renewed interest in this field. I don't claim to have any special knowledge or secret wisdom other than that which the Holy Spirit can give in any way He chooses. I'm not claiming that my interpretations are always Spirit-led; what I am claiming is that the Lord is choosing to speak to many by this means. It is wrong for us to not speak up about this for fear of what others will think or because they don't agree that God still works this way.

Many have a hard time believing that God can use such ordinary vessels as you and me to pour out His Holy Spirit. As you read the following pages, ask the Lord to open the eyes of your understanding so that you may know the hope of His calling and the riches of His inheritance that He has for you in Christ.

> *That the God of our Lord Jesus Christ, the Father of glory, may give unto* ______ (your name) *the spirit of wisdom and revelation in the knowledge of Him: the eyes of* ____ (your name) *understanding being enlightened; that* _____ (your name) *may know what is the hope of His calling, and what the riches of the glory of His inheritance in the saints* (Ephesians 1:17-18).

Pray this as a prayer for yourself, your neighbors, and your loved ones, and place your name and their names in the spaces. The Lord wants to open your eyes so that you may receive all He has for you. You have been bought and paid for by Christ's atonement, and even before the world began God ordained for you to hear His message.

Introduction

Most of what I will be sharing in this book is a series of dreams. Each was given for a particular reason, and only the reader can decide for himself what he believes the Lord is showing him through them. Each dream followed a specific pattern, so I can assure you I didn't think them up on my own. Some must be interpreted, but most are very clear. I personally was not raised to believe that the Lord speaks in dreams, but those of us who claim to believe the Word of God need to take a closer look at the life of Joseph.

Joseph was given some incredible dreams as a young man. When he told his brothers about the dreams he was having, they became quite upset. Joseph told his brothers about bundles of wheat, as well as the sun, the moon, and 11 stars, bowing down before him (see Gen. 37:5-10). By this time, even his own father rebuked him. Later, however, his father Jacob considered the matter, just as Mary pondered the things concerning Jesus over and over again in her heart (see Gen. 37:11; Lk. 2:19). It is very important that we also "consider the matter" and "ponder" these things first, before we wrongly judge someone who has truly been given a dream by the Spirit of the Lord.

I admit that some of the dreams and visions I've received might sound a little unusual, but try explaining how the sun and the moon can bow before you in a dream before you decide to judge something that you have never experienced yourself. It says in Psalm 105:19b that "the word of the Lord tried him" until his dreams came to pass. If you have a true God-given dream, it will be tested and tried, as in Joseph's case. But be encouraged by the fact that if God gave you the dream, then He will bring it to pass at its proper time.

It also says in Job that God speaks through dreams to protect man and keep him from his own pride.

> *For God speaketh once, yea twice, yet man perceiveth it not. In a dream, in a vision of the night, when deep sleep falleth upon men, in slumberings upon the bed; then He openeth the ears of men, and sealeth their instruction, that He may withdraw man from his purpose, and hide pride from man* (Job 33:14-17).

Many of the dreams I share in this book were very clear to me. They came about because the hand of the Lord was upon me at the time. Most of the dreams I share were followed by a sense of strong anointing when I awoke. The dreams in Chapters One and Two both followed the same pattern. I found myself waking up and climbing out of bed, even though I was still in my dream asleep. I then was given the choice to observe, as well as participate, while they were taking place.

Many of the dreams are symbolic and parabolic; they relate to specific areas we all go through in our lives. God has used these in my life many times to guide me, warn me, and direct me toward my own personal destiny. Some of my dreams were more personal; therefore, I will not share these in detail with the reader so as to maintain the confidentiality of those to whom the dreams referred. But I can state that one dream helped to bring a marriage back together, and another enabled a potentially serious accident to be avoided.

Some dreams simply gave assurance to specific people that the Lord loved them and was watching over them, and that even though they were going through a difficult time, the Lord would bring them out of their troubles and deliver them. Even the church I presently attend was revealed to me in a dream, as well as many other things that I will explain in further detail in Volume II. I have also included a short appendix at the end of this book about the testing and interpreting of dreams and the importance of honesty and integrity regarding these matters.

Some of the dreams, visions, and words, and even a song I have written about in this book, were given by God as a revelation to the entire Body of Christ to edify us and to exhort us to continue in the work He has called us to do. I believe that we shouldn't place so much emphasis on dreams that we use them to establish doctrines or exalt them above the Word of God, but we should be open to these revelations and use them for the purpose for which they were given.

Dreams and visions are intended to point us to God's Word and to direct us to the One who alone gives life to all who call upon His name. Let us follow the Spirit's leading and place our confidence and hope in Jesus, who alone is worthy of receiving our all in all and of fulfilling all our dreams and the desires of every heart.

Chapter One

Destined to Build the Father's House

And He taught, saying unto them, Is it not written, My house shall be called of all nations the house of prayer? but ye have made it a den of thieves (Mark 11:17).

And when He had made a scourge of small cords, He drove them all out of the temple, and the sheep, and the oxen; and poured out the changers' money, and overthrew the tables (John 2:15).

For the time is come that judgment must begin at the house of God: and if it first begin at us, what shall the end be of them that obey not the gospel of God? (1 Peter 4:17)

And now, Israel, what doth the Lord thy God require of thee, but to fear the Lord thy God, to walk in all His ways, and to love Him, and to serve the Lord thy God with all thy heart and with all thy soul (Deuteronomy 10:12).

I was given a dream many years ago that related to the building of my Father's house. Just as Christ declared when

He drove out those who sold doves in the temple, the Lord still wants His house to be a house of prayer that accepts all those whose hearts are longing to know and worship Him.

I believe that the following dream was given so that I might wake up and start to watch my own walk with the Lord. Yet I believe it is also a warning to all those who have been motivated by things other than a love for our God (see Mt. 22:37). Jesus said that many would come in His name in the last days and deceive many (see Mt. 24:5). Just because something is done in God's name doesn't necessarily mean that it originated from Him.

This is the first dream I ever wrote down or recorded. To this day, I can still remember certain dreams as clearly as when I was first given them. After I had this dream, I immediately wrote it down. I kept it to myself believing that one day I would understand its full meaning and its application. I have done my best to do just that. Here is the first dream in its entirety.

My Father's House

> *Then came the word of the Lord by Haggai the prophet, saying, Is it time for you, O ye, to dwell in your ceiled houses, and this house lie waste? Now therefore thus saith the Lord of hosts;* ***Consider your ways****. Ye have sown much, and bring in little; ye eat, but ye have not enough; ye drink, but ye are not filled with drink; ye clothe you, but there is none warm; and he that earneth wages earneth wages to put it into a bag with holes. Thus saith the Lord of hosts; Consider your ways. Go up to the mountain, and bring wood, and* ***build the house****; and I will take pleasure in it, and I will be glorified, saith the Lord* (Haggai 1:3-8).

I saw that my earthly father's house needed a lot of work. Some workers were supposed to come and help rebuild my father's house. He had called them to do the work, but when they kept making excuses, he decided that he would make other plans. When the day originally scheduled for the work to be done came, he was away. While I was asleep in my father's house, some workers came anyway. I got out of my bed and ran out to find out why they were here. I asked them if my father had contacted them again. They said that he had, but they seemed to avoid giving a straight answer.

At first, I didn't know who they were. Some of them with darker skin started to work. Then before my eyes, I saw their skin change color. I then recognized that some of them were old friends of mine. As I talked to them, they continued to work, assuring me that they knew what they were doing. I went back into the house and watched them work.

I entered a room where they kept many of their tools. Their tools were brand-new and had clearly been expensive. Even though they had all the proper tools to do the job, they didn't seem to be using many of them. I went back outside to watch them work. Instead of the few who had been working, there were now many, many more. I saw little children all around, and the more the workers multiplied, the less the work seemed to get done.

The next scene I remember was that the inside of my earthly father's house became the inside of a Christian church with benches all in rows. They were filled with people, and even though things settled down a bit inside, some of the children still played around outside. Soon some of the workers and others gathered together and began to sing beautiful Christian music.

It was at this moment in my dream that I realized all this had been just a dream and that my head had never left my pillow. I made a decision that since this was my dream, I might as well participate in it. I then, as part of my dream, woke myself up and climbed out of my bed, which was upstairs, and looked out over a ledge on the upper porch. As I looked, I could see many things still happening, both outside in the yard and inside as people began to fill the room. Yet the work that they were supposed to finish outside was left undone and in worse shape than ever.

I then decided to climb down and join those who were seated inside on the benches in my father's house. I chose the furthest seat on the left side and tried to remain unnoticed. I heard some of the people begin to repeat strange sounding prayers many times over and over in Jesus' name. One of them asked me if I would like to pray. I didn't want to stand out, so I prayed as I had heard others do.

Another recognized me and knew that it was my father's house we were in, but he expressed to me that he wouldn't say anything. Word seemed to have gotten out that my father was on his way back, so many left the gathering and started working again. Yet the more they worked, the worse things became.

I left the bench and walked back into the room with the tools and their containers. Many of the tools that had been used were ruined. Tools that once had bristles now had all the bristles pulled out and couldn't be used to sweep with. Other tools were just lying around, having been left in other than their proper places. Some tools were broken into pieces, now being completely useless for the purpose for which they had been designed.

My father was supposed to return home very shortly, and it now seemed that many of the workers knew it. While some still worked, others were supposed to be cleaning up and putting away the tools that were not in use. I began to put some of the tools back into their containers, and no one else even entered into the same room. I'm sure many began to realize that not all their motivations were right. Some did the work only for the money promised to them by others. Some came for other reasons, but it appeared that few were there because of their love for my dad and their desire to take part in the work.

Well, my father finally came home and was not pleased at all as he looked at what had been done to his house. Both the house and the yard were a complete wreck. The first thing he did was remove many who were upstairs, and by the time that was done, some others went out on their own, leaving their tools behind. While I watched my father, I thought to myself, *If only I had first called on my father, we never would have made such havoc of my father's house.*

Called to Build

At the time of this dream, my dad was actually having some work done on our house. He had never really taught me about building things or about mechanical things—I suppose his dad probably never taught him either—and even to this very day, I feel terribly inadequate when it comes to these areas of life. (It is important for fathers to pass on to their children some type of special skill or knowledge to prepare them for the future.) At the time of this work, even though I was Dad's son and should have been one to help, I wasn't yet trained in those areas.

Usually my father paid someone to come in and do the household work that required any type of technical knowledge. Although a hired worker can do good work, he generally doesn't have the same love for the work or care of the finished project as someone who actually shares in the results. When his work is done, he simply leaves and goes back to his own house.

A son, however, would not only be one to help build his father's house, but he would then stay there until he is old enough to get out on his own. In Malachi 4:6 the Lord says that He will turn the hearts of the children back again to their fathers and the hearts of the fathers to their children. Since God is our Father, should not our hearts be turning back to Him, and should not we desire to be involved in the building of His house?

In John 10:12-13 Jesus talks about the hireling. He will take care of the sheep and will do his job fine for awhile; but if a wolf comes, he will be much more concerned about his own neck than the safety of the sheep that are not his. My father's actions in the dream may sound a bit harsh to some, but I believe that the Lord was saying that judgment must begin first in His own house. This is in order that we can be prepared to help the rest of our brothers and sisters who are still out there in the world. Many still have not made it back to the Father's house. God wants to make sure that when they do return, they find a place where they can experience His love and forgiveness and can be restored into who and what they were meant to be.

The Lord doesn't want just another corporation that hires more workers for a task that they don't even enjoy being involved with. Building His house should be the joy of our hearts. The Lord wants His own children, those who have a love relationship with Him, to be the ones to build

His house. This is to be our highest calling as members of His family. This is our true purpose and destiny.

Watch Your Motivations

I noticed in the dream that some of the workers were old friends of mine, many of whom I hadn't seen in years. I knew in my dream that they cared little about my father or our family, and that some were just putting up a front.

I also noticed in the dream that some of the people changed color. They went from dark to light. This could have meant several things. It could have meant that they became born again and now had the light of Christ in them. Or it could have represented an outward image that was painted on without an inward change of the heart.

As Christians, many of us have learned how to put on a good face. Now, if we can put on a face so well, how about the world around us? The Scriptures declare that there are those whose god is their stomach and who keep their minds only on earthly things and care nothing for the work of the Lord (see Phil. 3:19). Jesus said we would know them by their fruit (see Lk. 6:44).

The Scriptures also declare that satan can transform himself into a minister of light, so don't think that those who follow his ways haven't learned many of his same methods (see 2 Cor. 11:13-15). Real Christians who love the Lord aren't perfect, but it is obvious that a change has taken place in their lives. The Scriptures themselves bear out this truth.

> *Therefore if any man be in Christ, he is a new creature: old things are passed away; behold, all things are become new* (2 Corinthians 5:17).

There were those in my dream who had no true inner change. I knew that many of them didn't care about my Father or about His house. Jesus made it clear that there were those in His day who didn't either. As you can see in the dream, I was in my bed asleep when the workers came. I believe that the Lord wanted me to wake up to see what was actually taking place in His house.

Sometimes the Lord has given me an anointing to know things I couldn't possibly have knowledge of. Ezekiel 40:4 (TLB) says:

> *He said to me: "Son of dust, watch and listen and take to heart everything I show you, for you have been brought here so I can show you many things; and then you are to return to the people of Israel to tell them all you have seen."*

Often, our motivations have not been right. I know—because the Lord has had to deal with me about this on more than one occasion. Many times I have put on a face without letting someone know my true heart. While some of us know the deceptions in our own hearts, others are simply ignorant of the reasons why they do the things they do (see Rom. 7:15).

We've all blown it time and again. Each of us needs to realize that forgiveness is available to us from the One who said, "Father, forgive them; for they know not what they do" (Lk. 23:34b). After my dream, I found it easy, at first, to exclude myself from this rebuke since it was my own father's house, but I was the one who through lack of knowing what to do had to be given the wake-up call. If I would have called on my heavenly Father through prayer, I probably could have become involved with the work of His house much earlier. The image of being asleep could also reveal a shallow prayer life. In my dream, though, I did finally wake up and desire to participate in the building of my Father's house.

> *And that, knowing the time, that now* ***it is high time to awake out of sleep****: for now is our salvation nearer than when we believed* (Romans 13:11).

God is giving each of us a wake-up call. It is time that we start to work together with all our brothers and sisters. The color of their skin doesn't matter; it's the color of their hearts that is important. We must not allow any racial walls to separate us. Black or white, red or yellow, all of us have been called to take part in the construction of our Father's house. We've each been given the ministry to reconcile men and women back to Him. This is our calling, and this is our purpose.

God has given us the Holy Spirit and His Word to help us carry this out. The Holy Spirit knows all the plans and details, as well as what the final outcome will be. He desires to instruct us and to help us bring our dreams together to see the house completed in love. The Lord doesn't mind all our imperfections and human tendencies, but He is concerned about what motivates us and the care that goes into our work.

Quality Work

> *According to the grace of God which is given unto me, as a wise masterbuilder, I have laid the foundation, and another buildeth thereon. But let every man take heed how he buildeth thereupon. For other foundation can no man lay than that is laid, which is Jesus Christ. Now if any man build upon this foundation gold, silver, precious stones, wood, hay, stubble;* ***every man's work shall be made manifest****: for the day shall declare it, because it shall*

> *be revealed by fire; and the fire shall try every man's work of what sort it is. If any man's work abide which he hath built thereupon, he shall receive a reward. If any man's work shall be burned, he shall suffer loss: but he himself shall be saved; yet so as by fire* (1 Corinthians 3:10-15).

I know that I still have quite a lot to work out in my life, as I'm sure you do, too. My prayer is that we all would take our responsibility as seriously as the Lord takes it. If we do, we will experience an even greater level of joy, knowing that we have done our best for Him.

> *But let every man prove his own work, and then shall he have* ***rejoicing in himself alone****, and not in another. For every man shall bear his own burden* (Galatians 6:4-5).

If we love the Lord, we will be concerned about seeing His house built by His blueprints and design. Our Father's house is to be a house built with love and made up of all kinds of people. Our God is a God of diversity. He doesn't want us all to be the same. It is in our coming together with all our differences and in our loving one another that true unity is created. God's house is to be a house of living stones chosen from every nation under the sun. In First Peter 2:5 (TLB) it says:

> *And now you have become living building-stones for God's use in building His house. What's more, you are His holy priests; so come to Him–[you who are acceptable to Him because of Jesus Christ]–and offer to God those things that please Him.*

God's house is to be built for people of all nations to come and worship Him. God wants His house to be in our hearts and in our homes. We should build His house for His glory alone.

> *But seek ye first the kingdom of God, and His righteousness; and all these things shall be added unto you* (Matthew 6:33).

Our first priority is to seek God and the things that relate to the building of His Kingdom. Everything else is to follow this. Many of us wonder sometimes why certain things in our lives are not working out like we think they should. God promises us that if we will put the things that concern Him first in our lives, He will take care of adding everything else. In other words, if we build His house, He will build ours.

Doing Our Part

Once I was in my front room, and I was building a house with wood sticks. My children wanted to help, and I wanted them to have the joy of being involved as well. All I asked them to do was to work nicely together and to hand me the sticks one at a time so that I could place them where they needed to go in the house.

Everything worked fine as each did his part, but pretty soon they started fighting among themselves. They started to place the sticks wherever they wanted them to go, without paying attention to anything I was trying to tell them. They ended up making an incredible mess. Finally, they knocked the house down, and I had to start over again.

Jesus has a special place for each of us. The Holy Spirit knows exactly where we fit. If we love the Lord, we will let Him place us and others where He wants us. Jesus said that He would build His house and the gates of hell would not prevail against it (see Mt. 16:18).

Let's not do His job, but let's participate with Him as fellow laborers who follow His plan. Consider Christ's words to Peter in John 21:15-17: Jesus asked Peter a very direct question, "Do you love Me?" Peter responded, "You know that I do, Lord." Jesus said to him, "Feed My sheep!"

I think it would be very difficult to face my Lord on the day of judgment knowing that I never took the time to help even one person come to know Him. Building His house is to be a family affair. How can we claim to love Him if we're not concerned about our brothers and sisters and we don't desire to help build His house?

> *Not everyone that saith unto Me, Lord, Lord, shall enter the kingdom of heaven; but he that doeth the will of My Father which is in heaven* (Matthew 7:21).

> *Don't you realize that all of you together are the house of God, and that the Spirit of God lives among you in His house? If anyone defiles and spoils God's home, God will destroy him. For God's home is holy and clean, and you are that home* (1 Corinthians 3:16-17 TLB).

Let's build our Father's house with the love of Jesus. Let's embrace all those who seek refuge in Him. Many are wounded and hurting and are in need of restoration. They need a place to come where they will receive God's love and forgiveness and where they will be accepted. He is not expecting us to do a perfect job, but He does want us to work with a heart motivated by our love for Him. God wants to stir us up to work in rebuilding His house. He will be with us if we desire to be involved in its restoration (see Hag. 1:13-14). He promises to restore it to its former glory and beyond:

> *The glory of this latter house shall be greater than of the former, saith the Lord of hosts: and in this place will I give peace, saith the Lord of hosts* (Haggai 2:9).

Don't mind the mess while our Father's house is being built. Just grab a board and hand it to Him. He knows exactly where to place it. He is not only making us a beautiful home to dwell in with our brothers and sisters on this earth, but He is also preparing our home in Heaven, which will be our eternal dwelling place with Him.

> *And I saw no temple therein: for the Lord God Almighty and the Lamb are the temple of it. And the city had no need of the sun, neither of the moon, to shine in it: for the glory of God did lighten it, and the Lamb is the light thereof. And the nations of them which are saved shall walk in the light of it: and the kings of the earth do bring their glory and honour into it* (Revelation 21:22-24).

> *In My Father's house are many mansions: if it were not so, I would have told you. I go to prepare a place for you* (John 14:2).

* * *

Father, thank You for allowing us, Your children, to be involved in the building of Your house. Wake each of us out of our "prayerlessness" and cause our prayers to ascend before Your throne. We give You full permission to enter our lives and cleanse us of all our pride and selfish ambition.

Help us learn to serve, praise, and worship You with a pure heart, in spirit and in truth, and deliver us from our traditions and from idle lip service. Help us to see our differences as something wonderful, and show us how we can come together in unity.

Jesus, thank You for placing us in Your body where You see fit. Teach us how to use the tools You've given to us instead of setting them aside because of our lack of knowledge.

Holy Spirit, cause us to see our brothers and sisters, regardless of race or color, with Your eyes. Help us each to recognize our role in encouraging those whose hearts yearn to know and love You. Build us into Your holy temple as those living stones set in the place that You've chosen for us so that we can glorify You alone. Amen.

Chapter Two

"These Children Shall Be Born"

> *That is what the Scriptures mean when they say that God made Abraham the father of many nations. God will accept all people in every nation who trust God as Abraham did. And this promise is from God Himself, who makes the dead live again and speaks of future events with as much certainty as though they were already past. So, when God told Abraham that He would give him a son who would have many descendants and become a great nation, Abraham believed God even though such a promise just couldn't come to pass!* (Romans 4:17-18 TLB)

The Lord gave Abraham a wonderful promise—that through his seed *all the families of the earth would be blessed.* This promise was to include people from every nation. It says in Romans 4:3, "Abraham believed God and it was counted unto him for righteousness." Mary, the mother of Jesus, was also given this same promise concerning the seed in her womb:

And the angel said unto her, Fear not, Mary: for thou hast found favour with God. And, behold, thou shalt conceive in thy womb, and bring forth a son, and shalt call His name Jesus (Luke 1:30-31).

Later, when Elizabeth heard Mary's greeting, the baby in her own womb leaped for joy (see Lk. 1:42-45). John the Baptist responded in this way because he was filled with the Holy Spirit inside his mother's womb, long before he was born. These examples prove that God calls many before they are ever born. Isaac and John were not just fetuses; they were known by God from their mothers' wombs.

The prophet Samuel was born not only as a result of Hannah's prayer to have a child but also out of God's desire to raise up a prophet who would speak for Him:

And she vowed a vow, and said, O Lord of hosts, if Thou wilt indeed look on the affliction of Thine handmaid, and remember me, and not forget Thine handmaid, but wilt give unto Thine handmaid a man child, then I will give him unto the Lord all the days of his life, and there shall no razor come upon his head (1 Samuel 1:11).

The Lord opened Hannah's womb as an answer to this request. The name *Samuel* means "asked of the Lord." Many adoption agencies are very busy with the requests of those who desire to have children to call their own but who haven't been able to conceive. Our intense, natural desire to have children correlates with God's desire to have each of us as His child. The Scriptures teach that those who are born only according to the flesh are not the children of God. Romans 9:8-9 (TLB) says:

This means that not all of Abraham's children are children of God, but only ***those who believe the promise of***

> ***salvation*** *which He made to Abraham. For God had promised, "Next year I will give you and Sarah a son."*

Jesus said in John 3:5-7 that you *must be born again* to enter the Kingdom of Heaven. *Are you planning to go to Heaven?* Do you know what it means to be born again? Only those with simple, childlike faith in God's promises can accept that their own works can't save them and that they need a *new birth* to become a member of God's family and receive the right to build His house.

God is not willing that even one person should perish without knowing Him as Father (see 2 Pet. 3:9). It is not the Father's will that even one little child should perish without Him (see Mt 18:14).

The Wrong Appointment

When I was a child, I saw a calendar about the dreams and plans of a baby still in his mother's womb. He talked about his different body parts as they grew, and his excitement increased over being prepared by God to be ready to live in the world as an integral member of society. He talked about his strong arms and how one day he might become a football player or possibly play piano or be a carpenter.

As each day drew closer to the time of his birth, his excitement continued to grow. He dreamed, planned, and schemed of all he was going to do in the world upon his arrival. When his due date finally arrived, the calendar read: "Doctor Appointment." He thought to himself, *I wonder if this could be the day of my birth?* However, it was on that date of the calendar that his mother had scheduled an abortion.

God is "pro-life." It is the only way He can be. I once read a bumper sticker that read: "Aren't you glad your mother was pro-life?" Well, I certainly am. I believe that our children should be given the chance of life, just as we were.

We complain about all the problems in our society and how wicked it has become. Maybe the very children who were to be born endowed by the grace of God with those gifts necessary to help the human condition never came into our world because they were aborted–and their gifts along with them. Abortion is so sad because it makes the statement that human life is cheap. Convenience silently murders the innocent, and man ends up playing God, entirely unaware of the greater purposes of our Creator's plans.

Children represent many things. They represent all our hopes and dreams. They represent new beginnings as we pass on the sword of God's Word from one generation to the next. The Bible states in Psalm 127:3-5 (TLB) what is God's own heart toward our children. Just listen:

> *Children are a gift from God; they are His reward. Children born to a young man are like sharp arrows to defend him. Happy is the man who has his quiver full of them. That man shall have the help he needs when arguing with his enemies.*

I never planned to be writing a chapter like this. In fact, by the time I was a teenager I had begun to think just like the world and sometimes wished I had never been born. Even though I had a mom and dad who loved me, I still felt rejected and unloved. I didn't understand or believe that I had any purpose, or that my life mattered to anyone. I didn't know at that time about the Savior who gave His life for me and who considered me more valuable than all the riches of this world. I had no idea just how much He really loved me.

The Root Cause

Abortion, as bad as it is, is still not the cause or root; it is only the symptom of a disease that affects many. Blocking abortion clinics and protesting against the ideas of the abortionists certainly do prevent many individual abortions, but this will not solve the problem. Only if we get to the true root (especially among the Body of Christ) can we truly affect the rest of the world.

Jesus said that we are to love God with our whole heart, soul, mind, and strength, and our neighbor as ourselves (see Mt. 22:37-40). Love does not harm his neighbor. If we truly love God and believe that He loves us, it isn't so hard for us to love ourselves. We then have less of a problem really loving others and being able to see the beauty and value of each human soul, which is precious to the very heart of God. Scripture instructs us:

> *Next, learn to put aside your own desires so that you will become patient and godly, gladly letting God have His way with you. This will make possible the next step, which is for you to enjoy other people* [and your children too] *and to like them, and finally you will grow to love them deeply. The more you go on in this way, the more you will grow strong spiritually and become fruitful and useful to our Lord Jesus Christ* (2 Peter 1:6-8 TLB).

If we love God, we will love His Word, and His Word clearly teaches us the sanctity of human life. He shows us that each life is very dear to His heart and that each one of us is precious to Him. Based upon my past feelings or experience, I would appear to be unqualified to write this book. Yet I believe that the Lord qualifies us not only by our schooling or education but also by His Spirit and His own instruction.

Whether or not you believe in dreams is not much of an issue to me. Yet because I grew up not believing in dreams, visions, or prophetic words I can truly relate if you're still not too sure the Lord can speak to us by this means. Today, however, I am a firm believer in such things because of my personal experiences and because I have seen many of them come to pass. Indeed, you would not be reading this today had it not been for a dream the Lord gave me when I was a young man.

It says in Joel 2:28 that prophecies, dreams, and visions are major ways the Lord will communicate with His people in the last days. Had it not been for these means, I'm sure our Bibles would be much smaller. Although I was not raised to believe in such things, the Lord chose a very interesting and startling way to reveal these truths to me. He gave me a dream, a vision, and prophetic words all in one night.

The Lord can do and act as He pleases. While we should never base our doctrine on these matters, we should keep an open ear and a discerning heart to hear whatever the Lord has to say, no matter how He chooses to speak—especially in these last days. Some who don't believe that the Lord can work this way may be quite surprised when He starts working this way in them or in someone close to them.

Has God been speaking this way to you? Have you been hearing His voice? Jesus said in John 10:27, "My sheep hear My voice, and I know them, and they follow Me."

I believe that the Lord will soon start to give us His guidance from Heaven by many different means. I believe that He is beginning to speak clearly again to men and women to give His solutions and answers to many of the problems we face. I know how ignorant I can be at times.

Often it has been the Lord's wisdom and not my own that has gotten me "out of the soup."

I believe that some of the most critical issues in our society could be solved with just one word from Heaven. The question is, Would we believe a person who claimed to have this heavenly source, or would we side with satan by persecuting the individual and dismissing his ideas and thoughts instead of encouraging them?

Each of us, as individuals, needs to continue to seek the One who alone contains and holds the universe in His hands. He is the One who made everything that can be seen, as well as everything unseen. Since He is the Maker of all things, He knows how everything works and where each piece fits.

I believe that God has an ultimate dream. From time to time He gives one or more of us a piece of that dream. If we know only one part of the whole, it's hard to see what the final outcome will be; but as we come together and start to lay each piece side by side on the table, we will be able to see the whole picture. Some pieces may still be hidden under the sofa, but when they are all found, we will see the beautiful picture God has planned.

God wants each one of us to fulfill the dreams He has given us. Without the piece He has given me or you, the picture is incomplete. So this dream the Lord gave me one night may seem small and insignificant, but I believe that it has set the rudder for other things that never would have occurred had I not had it.

Seeing Stars

I want to first give you a little background that will help you understand the dream that I was given. My bedroom was a converted second garage. I had to be moved downstairs because my Grandmother Merle and my Uncle Guy had come to live with us. My grandmother took my sister Brenda's old room, and my sister ended up with my room. My father, Bruce Druckenmiller, had the inside of the garage converted into my bedroom. Because there were no windows, it was pitch black all the time unless a light was on.

In my dream I woke up in the middle of the night and noticed light coming into my room. I didn't know I was dreaming, but actually thought it was taking place. I didn't remember anyone ever putting a window in my room, but I thought that maybe my dad put one in to surprise me. It was all so real to me.

Well, I climbed out of my bed and walked over to the window to see what the light was. To my utter amazement, I realized that I was seeing stars. What was really bizarre is that they were not only up in the sky, but also down below. As far as the eye could see, I saw stars, and then in the middle of the stars I saw a planet that looked like Earth.

Then, a most amazing thing occurred. A power welled up on the inside of me, and I found myself yelling with all the strength within me through a power I could tell was not from myself. As my words flung out over space, I felt that they were filled with power that could change things around me, and it seemed that they were directed toward that little planet in front of me. These were the words that I spoke out of my window across the universe: ***"Thus says the Lord, 'These children shall be born.' "*** These were words from Heaven that were anointed with God's power.

Now you must agree that this was very unusual, to say the least. When my wife and I first met, she told me that she couldn't have children. After her previous marriage, Sue decided that she didn't want to have more children, so she had an operation to tie her fallopian tubes so that she would never again become pregnant. I was troubled at Sue's lack of desire to have more children, but the Lord had clearly shown me that Sue was the one He had chosen to be my wife.

To make a long story short, Sue and I now have three children: Joshua (my stepson), Daniel, and Karis. With the special help of a Jewish doctor, Dr. Barry Witten of St. John's Hospital in St. Louis, Sue underwent a successful tubular reversal operation, and about two months later she became pregnant with our first child, Daniel. Two years later, Karis was born. Her name is the Greek word for "favor," or God's grace. *Karis* is the word the angel used when he told Mary that she had found "favor" in God's sight.

Just like my wife needed an operation before she could give birth, so also the Bride of Christ (the Church) is in need of an operation. The Holy Spirit is entering the womb and causing children who have the "favor" of God to be birthed once again.

Judgment and Grace

One time as I was preparing for a teaching about the word *grace,* I noticed the word *karis* in my concordance. When I saw *karis,* I said to myself that it looked like it could be a girl's name, so I wrote it in the corner of my Bible and didn't think much about it. When Sue and I started dating, I told her that I thought we would have two children of our own.

She wrote a poem to me one time, mentioning both of our children. I still have the original. Here is a small portion of the poem Sue wrote:

> "...holding a baby girl and boy with red eyelashes and hair that have his eyes on a sunny afternoon; running

down a mountaintop on a snowy day with Bart "daddy," little Karis and Daniel on a sled made for a family of God. Holding our first baby to my breast as I gaze into her sweet little eyes with tears of joy..."

I included this because it was written before we were even married, and Sue did not yet have the ability to conceive. Both our children were named before they were born. For some reason I always thought that I would have two children of my own. I thought my first child would represent God's grace and my second child would represent God's judgment. The name *Daniel* means "God is Judge," or the "judgment of God."

However, Daniel was born first. When Sue became pregnant after her operation, everyone thought that the child would be a girl. This was clearly in the poem Sue wrote. Also, after the ultrasound, the person who ran the test told us that she thought the child would be a girl.

However, about a month before our first child was born, I had a dream. I saw a little baby boy with red hair completely submerged under water. I even had the thought while looking at him in the dream that he had my father's features. When I awoke I told my wife, as well as a couple in our new church. I believe the Lord allowed me to actually see Daniel before he was born. This little boy wasn't just a fetus. *Daniel was known by the Lord* while still in his mother's womb.

When I read Jeremiah 1:5 (TLB), it still gives me shivers:

> *I knew you before you were formed within your mother's womb; before you were born I sanctified you and appointed you as My spokesman to the world.*

Giving Birth

According to the Scriptures, judgment (Daniel) begins first at the house of God (see 1 Pet. 4:17). Only then can He pour out His grace (Karis) upon us. There is a seed that is known by God and called from the womb that God declares "shall be born." Psalm 139 says that we were carefully formed in our mother's womb and all our days were known before we had any.

Now you can know the importance of understanding God's prophecy to satan in Genesis 3:15 (TLB):

> *From now on you and the woman will be enemies, as will all of your offspring* [seed] *and hers. And I will put the fear of you into the woman, and between your offspring and hers. He shall strike you on your head, while you will strike at his heel.*

Satan worked through Herod behind the scenes–just like he did when Moses was born–to attempt to stop "the seed of the woman" from being able to live and breathe on this earth. Christ's birth was God's promise of restoration to Adam after his fall in the garden. This is why the Word had to become flesh (see Jn. 1:14). Since no man on earth could be a perfect sacrifice to pay the price for mankind's full redemption from sin, the Lord Himself had to come down from Heaven into our world in the person of Christ to restore fallen humanity.

> *For what the law could not do, in that it was weak through the flesh, God sending His own Son in the likeness of sinful flesh, and for sin, condemned sin in the flesh* (Romans 8:3).

God wanted to restore us to Himself through a spiritual rebirth and once again have us as His very own sons and daughters! The cross was the only means through which God could give us the right to be called His children once again. God wanted these children to be born. We are these children of promise, and that is *why we must be born again* to enter the Kingdom of Heaven. It is only through Christ's sacrifice on the cross and our receiving of His resurrection life that we have the right to call upon God as our very own Father.

> *And this is the record, that God hath given to us eternal life, and this life is in His Son. He that hath the Son hath life: and he that hath not the Son of God hath not life* (1 John 5:11-12).

This verse clearly states that if you have the Son, you have eternal life; and if you do not have the Son, you do not have eternal life. Those who have never been born again do not have this "life" in them. This means they can't legally call God their Father. It is impossible for anyone to begin to fulfill his God-given destiny until he first allows God to become his Father. This comes only through a spiritual birth, just like our first entrance into this world comes only by a natural birth.

I believe that the birth of children in our dreams represents not only people but also our dreams and desires. Many of us abort our dreams before they are ever born. Sometimes the labor pains become too intense and we believe that we can't take the pain, so we don't let the dream come forth. For whatever reason, the Lord is telling His Church that He doesn't want those desires aborted any longer.

We are in a serious time. It seems that the world around us is taking a turn for the worse. Dreams of a brighter future filled with the promises of God have been stolen from many people. Just looking at some of the events surrounding the current crises and wars in many countries around the world causes many of us to wonder if there is still hope for a better tomorrow.

As the children of God, we should understand that we were born for "such a time as this" (see Esth. 4:14). Just like Queen Esther, we have been placed in our world to make a difference in the midst of what seem to be impossible odds. Isaiah 37:3 (TLB) gives us a picture of what has been happening many times over in our world today.

> *They brought him this message from Hezekiah: "This is a day of trouble and frustration and blasphemy; it is a serious time, as when a woman is in heavy labor trying to give birth, and the child does not come."*

Picture a mother having carried twin children in her womb for nine months. She has her legs in the stirrups and is in labor. Just when the top of the first baby's head is seen, she suddenly relaxes and the child goes back in. She says she is too weak and tired, and then gives up and goes back home. What a sad picture this is, especially since her children are just ready to be born.

These children could have given the mom someone to love. They could have returned her love. Each one could have been a brother or sister to someone, a mom, a dad, an uncle, or an aunt. One could have become a minister or a doctor, yet the mother didn't have enough faith, strength, or support to bring them into the world. An entire generation that could have been born disappeared from the earth without ever having the chance to be manifested on our earth.

Because of our society and the stresses in our world today, the lack of marital and family support, and the social deterioration of ethics and morals, many women accept abortion as their only choice. Many have also felt compelled to make this decision because of a lack of hope due to extreme poverty or the fear of abandonment. This is a disheartening fact and a sad commentary on our generation.

Where there is godly sorrow and true repentance, the Lord shows great mercy and forgiveness toward those who have already had abortions. His restoration and healing are available to all who have felt trapped into this decision. Also, many believe that these children who were conceived in the womb yet never had the opportunity to live on this earth are already up in Heaven, waiting for us. So I encourage every woman who has had an abortion to receive the grace and forgiveness of God so that she can experience the joy of being reunited with her child one day.

For those women who are still considering abortion, allow me to affirm to you that adoption is always a better choice, and there are many other options too. The Lord will help you and sustain you if you will just trust Him and leave that precious little life in His hands.

An Aborted Dream

As I said before, these aborted children can also be viewed as pictures of aborted dreams. Also the mother could represent not only a solitary person but also a congregation, a country, or the Body of Christ as a whole. A great tragedy in the Church is that sons and daughters whom God destined to carry the message of Christ to the nations are being aborted just before they are ready to come into their time of fruitful ministry.

This can happen when a pastor no longer believes in or supports the young man or woman of God who is training for ministry. Out of discouragement, this young person may go back into the world and begin using his or her talents to gain wealth instead of souls. Or maybe a seminary or Bible school is no longer receiving adequate support from its denomination, and so the missionaries who were being trained had to abort their missions for lack of funds. For whatever reason, these children are being aborted and are becoming murdered dreams that have been placed in a grave and will therefore never come to fruition.

Whether the dream is for a country or a person, I believe that the Lord will work to help make it a reality if the dream is for the good of all and if it fits within His overall plan. My pastor says that it is better to at least try to give birth to a God-given dream and fall short than never to try at all.

Miracle Births

The Lord has given and is yet giving many publicized modern-day miracles to show us a prophetic picture of His will in this matter. Although there are many that I could list, I want to focus on just a few. It is said by many that each baby is proof that God still wants the world to go on.

In 1997, Bobbie McCaughey gave birth to seven children. Most of the world waited and watched to see what would happen to these famous septuplets. Even President Clinton called them on the day of their birth to congratulate them. This couple's pastor and church, as well as many others, prayed with the family.

Others, however, before the babies were born, suggested to the mother that she should use "selective reduction," which meant removing some of the babies from the womb, choosing which babies would live and which would die. I remember hearing Bobbie McCaughey say on TV that had she followed this advice, one day she would have to answer to God, and she wasn't going to be one to play God.

All seven children were born one minute apart between 12:48 p.m. and 12:54 p.m. on November 19, 1997. Another mother, Nkem Chukwu, gave birth to octuplets on December 8, 1998. She also refused to abort any of her children. Seven children in 1997! *Eight* children in 1998! God is making quite a point with these multiple births. Some people, I'm sure, would say that this is just another coincidence. I'm wondering if there are any ladies open to having nine children in 1999?!

I believe that it is of prophetic significance that the seventh child of the McCaughey septuplets was named Joel. The name *Joel* means "The Lord is his God." Joel 2:28 says that our sons and daughters shall prophesy. What a prophetic fulfillment! The births of these children prophesy God's will loud and clear that *all these children shall be born*. Joel is also the child who started to have complications toward the end. His parents made a statement that I thought was significant. They said, "Joel will be a fighter. He will fight his way back to the top."

Satan tries to stop dreams, but we need to fight before God's throne with unceasing prayer to see them come to pass. Joel was put on many churches' prayer chains and recovered very quickly. I believe that this was due to the many prayers and the fact that "the Lord is his God."

The last of the Chukwu octuplets was named Oderuh, which means "God has my life." He is the only one who didn't make his full entrance into our world. Since "God has his life," he is now safe up in Heaven with Jesus. We need to continue to pray for these little ones because some have had additional complications since their birth.

> *Behold, I and the children whom the Lord hath given me are for signs and for wonders in Israel from the Lord of hosts, which dwelleth in mount Zion* (Isaiah 8:18).

In essence, the Lord is telling our generation, "***These children shall be born.***" It was a miracle for Sarah to give birth to Isaac, and Isaac means laughter. Scripture tells us that the joy of the Lord is to be our strength (see Neh. 8:10). God has been pouring out His joy in increasing measure upon His Church. Isaac is a prophetic picture of the Father's joy of seeing His children born. Isaac was given to Abraham in answer to the promise that in his seed all the families of the earth would be blessed.

Now God is once again saying to us that He will give us the strength we need to overcome all adversity. He will give the strength of joy to those mothers who decide to once again bring forth children (and dreams). Now we can see why our enemy tries so hard to fight against us, or to get us to fight among ourselves. He wants to stop these children before they are born, and he wants to stop us from fulfilling our dreams.

> *And there appeared another wonder in heaven; and behold a great red dragon, having seven heads and ten horns, and seven crowns upon his heads. And his tail drew the third part of the stars of heaven, and did cast them to the earth: and the dragon stood before the woman which was ready to be delivered, for to devour her child as soon as it was born* (Revelation 12:3-4).

This Scripture gives a true picture of our enemy. He tries to stop a dream when it is small. He even tries to devour the child before it is birthed. This is what satan tried to do during the days of the births of Moses and of our

Lord. This is still his main agenda today among people, churches, and nations.

Another significant miracle occurred in Africa. In one of the issues of *Impact*, a publication of Reinhard Bonnke Ministries, Reinhard shared a miracle that occurred during a crusade. After he had prayed for healing, a mother came up to him and told him that when he had called out the name of Jesus, her baby had leaped in her womb.

Reinhard didn't understand why this woman was so excited until she showed him the hospital papers that declared her baby was dead in her womb and was to be removed the next day. Reinhard then told the mother that the child would be born that day, and that she should hurry home. After the mother arrived at her home, she gave birth to a beautiful healthy baby boy.

> *He maketh the barren woman to keep house, and to be a joyful mother of children. Praise ye the Lord* (Psalm 113:9).

On March 28, 1999, I was given a dream in which I found myself overhearing a conversation between a foreign man and woman about what name they would give to their new child. The woman kept saying that she wanted to name her baby "Merika" because she was thankful to be living in America.

I couldn't understand why I was given this dream since it did not seem to be related to anything going on in my life at the time. However, on the eleventh of May 1999, while watching the evening news, I received quite a shock. It was being reported that the first baby to be born to those coming over from Kosovo was being named "Amerikan." I also learned later that St. Louis was chosen to be one of the host cities to welcome many of them in.

I believe that the Lord gave me this dream as a prophetic picture of the fact that He knows each one of us by name and has destined even the time and place of our arrival. The examples I have given in this book are but signs in the earth of the sovereign work of God in our midst.

When my father was a baby, he was in a car accident that sent him through the front windshield of his parent's car, nearly killing him. I, too, almost died as an infant. A tumor that was blocking my breathing was found in my neck. I thank God for the doctors who removed it. I still have a three-inch scar on my neck that reminds me to be thankful for doctors and for the merciful and watchful care of God my Father. The devil comes only to steal, kill, and destroy, but our wonderful, precious Lord came to give us life and to give it to us "more abundantly" (see Jn. 10:10).

You are special to God, and your life is necessary, as is mine. We are children of destiny whom the Lord declared would be born. We are the seed that the Lord has hidden in this earth, and it is now time for us to rise up and declare our Father's wonderful plan. We are the purpose of all ages, created in our Father's image, and known and loved by Him.

The Apple of His Eye

The whole creation travails in birth awaiting the manifestation of the children of God–the unveiling of those who are the children of the King (see Rom. 8:19). You are born again of incorruptible seed. Your Father in Heaven loves you, and you are precious to Him. You are valuable, and you are the apple of His eye.

God said that Abraham would have a son. This was the promise. In effect, God was saying to him that "these children shall be born." I believe that God is saying this to our generation as well! As with Abraham, our "Isaacs" will be born because of our faith in God's promises and through our trusting Him to bring His word to pass at the appointed time.

God desires to see His promises birthed anew in our hearts. Ask the Lord to help you renew your vision. Ask Him to help you fulfill His promise for your life.

> *And Abraham's faith did not weaken, even though he knew that he was too old to be a father at the age of one hundred and that Sarah, his wife, had never been able to have children. Abraham never wavered in believing God's promise. In fact, his faith grew stronger, and in this he brought glory to God. He was absolutely convinced that God was able to do anything He promised* (Romans 4:19-21 NLT).

God called us into existence when we were not yet—before the world began. Ephesians 1:4-5 tells us that it was His good pleasure to have us as His own. We are the children He purposed to be born. Just look at His promise of a generation not yet born that would praise Him.

> *I am recording this so that future generations will also praise the Lord for all that He has done. And a people that shall be created shall praise the Lord* (Psalm 102:18 TLB).

Just as Sue and I wrote down our children's names before they were born, the Lord spoke this word through David and recorded it in the Psalms for all future generations. We are the children He has destined to praise Him. He created us for this purpose, and He has called each of us by name. Isn't it wonderful! *You and I were born for such a time as this.* The same promise God gave to Abraham He now gives to us. Children of God, come forth! The world waits for your manifestation. Thus says the Lord, "***These children shall be born!***"

Here is a beautiful poem written by Mary Ann Mercurio, one of the young adults who previously taught at Life Christian School.

God's Precious Jewels

Each and every one of these children is a precious jewel.
They hold a special spot in God's heart.
They are the colorful strings that weave together in God's heart.
Their eyes are the eyes of Jesus...full of compassion,
love, gentleness, kindness, purity, and innocence.
Each touch is a touch of gentleness.
Their stories are full of life and joy.
Their innocent voices that tell the stories are as sweet as honey.
Their laughter is full of joy and happiness.
God gave us children so that we can laugh and have fun.
Children put the sparkle in God's eye.
Their smile will light up the world.
They are the very essence of Jesus.
Children are God's creation, made in His own image.
God gave us this creation to teach and love.
It is an honor that He has bestowed into our lives.

"Jesus loves the little children, all the children of the world.
Red and yellow, black and white, they are precious in
His sight. Jesus loves the little children of the world."

* * *

Father, we need Your forgiveness for the abortions that have caused such pain and sorrow in our land. Convict us that we might never abort our children, our dreams, or our desires that You have placed in us. Thank You for the faith of our father Abraham, who believed Your promises and didn't doubt Your Word. Help us to raise our children with this same faith, to trust You in every situation. May we, as individuals, churches, and nations, work together to see Your children and Your dreams come forth once more.

Give us the faith of Mary who said, "Be it unto me according to Thy word" (see Lk. 1:38). Help us to become those children whom You have ordained to be born to praise You during such a difficult time as this. Thank You for allowing us to call You "Abba, Father!" and for believing in us as Your beloved children. Amen.

Chapter Three

"Let These Go Their Way"

Then opened He their understanding, that they might understand the scriptures, and said unto them, ***Thus it is written, and thus it behoved Christ to suffer, and to rise from the dead the third day: and that repentance and remission of sins should be preached in His name among all nations,*** *beginning at Jerusalem. And ye are witnesses of these things. And, behold, I send the promise of My Father upon you: but tarry ye in the city of Jerusalem, until ye be endued with power from on high* (Luke 24:45-49).

For John truly baptized with water; but ye shall be baptized with the Holy Ghost not many days hence. When they therefore were come together, they asked of Him, saying, Lord, wilt Thou at this time restore again the kingdom to Israel? And He said unto them, It is not for you to know the times or the seasons, which the Father hath put in His own power. ***But ye shall receive power, after that the Holy Ghost is come upon you:*** *and ye shall be witnesses unto Me both in Jerusalem, and in all Judaea, and in Samaria,* ***and unto the uttermost part of the earth*** (Acts 1:5-8).

At one time in my life, I believed that it really didn't matter much whether we believed in the ministry of the Holy Spirit or not, as long as we loved our fellow believers. However, the Lord later showed me through a series of circumstances that if I desired to grow spiritually and to fulfill His plan for my life, I would need to understand the ways of the Holy Spirit in a much greater way. He showed me that if I was ever to see things from the Book of Acts in my own life, I needed to understand and experience that which the early apostles had known.

John the Baptist said in Matthew 3:11 *that Jesus would baptize with the Holy Spirit and with fire.* Everyone is to experience the fire of Pentecost. The entire key to this revelation is not another formula, but a relationship with the Holy Spirit of the living God. We must allow Him full reign in our hearts and lives.

Pentecost at the Park

The following dream began on a bus. In the dream, I was standing up in the middle of the bus aisle and sharing the message of salvation with those on board. After a while, the bus stopped, and we all got out. We then proceeded to a park-like area where everyone started to climb up on different bleachers. Again, I started to share the Word.

I noticed that many of those who got off the bus with me showed very little interest in what I was saying and were talking to one another. I then opened my Bible and started reading Acts 2:1-4:

> *And when the day of Pentecost was fully come, they were all with one accord in one place. And suddenly there came a sound from heaven as of a rushing mighty wind, and it filled all the house where they were sitting. And there*

> *appeared unto them cloven tongues like as of fire, and it sat upon each of them. And they were all filled with the Holy Ghost, and began to speak with other tongues, as the Spirit gave them utterance.*

While I read these verses, I noticed something unusual. Every second person somehow shifted their bodies toward me and began to show excitement and interest on their faces. Those who were turned my way held Bibles in their laps and a pen and paper in their hands, and they were taking notes. Those who were not facing me kept looking at each other and continued to show very little interest in what I was trying to tell them. As I prepared to raise my voice at this second group–to get them to start paying attention–I heard a still, small voice say to me, "**Let these go their way.**" Those on the bleachers who were facing me were attentive and continued to read the Book of Acts with me. The others went their way–some to one bench and some to another.

There is a time for everything in our Christian walk. While I was on the bus, the message of salvation was being given; however, the Lord never intended for us to keep riding the same bus all our lives. We are to take what we have learned on the bus and share it with the world.

He desires to take us even further, for there are other realms of the Spirit and other rooms in His house that He wants to show us. There is a time to "take notes" and read, but there also comes a time to experience the fire of Pentecost for ourselves. Those in my dream who were taking notes were indicating their strong desire to learn all they could from the Word of God concerning the things of the Spirit.

Each one of us must have this type of attitude and hunger if we are to receive everything God has for us. In my dream, the Lord instructed me to focus my attention upon the ones who were hungry for the things of the Holy Spirit instead of spending all my time trying to convince those who weren't.

The dream also seemed to be telling me that once we are born again, we should immediately begin our new walk in the Spirit. God wants us to "get off the bench" and start living for Him. Pentecost is supposed to be real for each one of us, not just something we read about as a distant historical event. It should be our "next step" in our walk as a Christian. For a while God allows us to "take notes" at different benches, but there comes a designated time when He wants us to get off the bench and start to walk out our faith, just like the early disciples.

In my dream, those who turned away from me were not yet hungry enough to pay attention to God's Word. We need to support these persons as brothers and sisters, but we are not to follow their way. We need to go the way of the apostles. "Let these go their way" for now, until their hunger increases. We need to go to those who are hungry to know God now. The Lord might have these others "taking notes" at other benches for a time. Hopefully, they too will desire a fresh baptism and filling of the Holy Spirit and will experience the fire of Pentecost for themselves.

I believe that God wants to get His entire Church ready for what He is about to do. The message has now gone out that we are to meet our Bridegroom soon, and many still are not ready. Truly the Lord is starting to wake up many of us before we miss out on everything He has planned for us. Let's look at a parable Jesus told to illustrate this truth:

> *The Kingdom of Heaven can be illustrated by the story of ten bridesmaids who took their lamps and went to meet the*

> *bridegroom. But only five of them were wise enough to fill their lamps with oil, while the other five were foolish and forgot. So, when the bridegroom was delayed, they lay down to rest until midnight, when they were roused by the shout, "**The bridegroom is coming!** Come out and welcome him." All the girls jumped up and trimmed their lamps. Then the five who hadn't any oil begged the others to share with them, for their lamps were going out. But the others replied, "We haven't enough. Go instead to the shops and buy some for yourselves." But while they were gone, the bridegroom came, and those who were ready went in with him to the marriage feast, and the door was locked. Later, when the other five returned, they stood outside, calling, "Sir, open the door for us!" But he called back, "Go away! It is too late!"* ***So stay awake and be prepared, for you do not know the date or moment of My return*** (Matthew 25:1-13 TLB).

A fresh outpouring is taking place all over the world. The Lord has been awakening, reviving, renewing, restoring, reforming, and transforming His Church. We need the oil of the Holy Spirit as a fresh filling if we are to keep our lamps burning bright as we approach the "midnight hour." Ask the Holy Spirit to fill you with more oil. You will need it as time goes on. *Don't be found asleep when the Lord comes.*

If you're filled with oil (the Holy Spirit) and wisdom, He'll keep your lamp burning until He comes. Personally, I want to be one of the five wise virgins. I'm sure you do, too. To be among them, we must become hungry for God to move in ever greater ways in our lives, and we must not give up.

The Right Coat for the Journey

The senior pastors of Life Christian Center, Pastors Rick and Donna Shelton, have used the following illustration from a time when two of their sons went with them to a ball game. One son didn't dress warm enough and was freezing. The other son wore a sweatshirt and brought along a jacket suited for the type of weather for the day. One son was very cold and miserable, while the other son was warm and comfortable.

The son who was freezing finally begged his brother for the jacket he was wearing. The warmer son said to his father, "Dad, I prepared for today and dressed accordingly. It's not my fault that my brother didn't." This is what it will be like. Those who have been receiving the oil of the Holy Spirit will have the wisdom and the joy they will need, even during difficult times.

It is important to be prepared for what is coming upon our earth. It says in Hebrews that God will shake everything that can be shaken (see Heb. 12:26).

I once had a dream in which I was following a little white dove. It looked small and insignificant, until it started to fly next to some large buildings. As it did, these buildings started to crumble and crash to the ground. I then saw the dove fly right into one of these stone structures and disappear. Suddenly buildings began to collapse all around, and the ground rumbled. I saw devastation everywhere. I saw tall trees uprooted and lying in rows all over the ground.

As this was going on around me, I ended up following a small path to a group of people who were waiting in a line. There were two men of God at the front of the line laying hands on each person as he passed. They were also checking the clothes the people wore. They wanted to see if their clothes were sufficient for the journey ahead.

Finally, I reached one of the men who was praying for the people. He looked at the clothes I was wearing. Then he did something I thought was quite unusual. He reached behind my neck to the inside of my collar and pulled out the label of the coat I had on. As soon as he looked, there was joy on his face, and he assured me that my coat would be sufficient for the journey.

Many people today are concerned about the name brand or label of their clothes. The Lord wants us to be clothed with His anointing, and with grace and humility. So first, let us put on the garment of salvation that Christ paid for on the cross. Then as we continue to seek Him, we will discover that there are also other "clothes" available for us to wear at times.

God compares the clothing of our own righteousness to filthy rags. When Adam and Eve sinned, they tried to clothe themselves with fig leaves. Their pious act of attempting to cover themselves only clothed them temporarily because their leaves couldn't remove their self-imposed guilt or cover their shame.

Only the blood shed from an innocent Lamb enabled God to clothe them (see Gen. 3:21). Jesus talks about this prepared garment of salvation in Matthew 22:11-13 (TLB):

> *But when the king came in to meet the guests he noticed a man who wasn't wearing the wedding robe [provided for him]. "Friend," he asked, "how does it happen that you are here without a wedding robe?" And the man had no reply. Then the king said to his aides, "Bind him hand and foot and throw him out into the outer darkness where there is weeping and gnashing of teeth."*

Jesus is presenting His Bride, the Church, to Himself without spot or wrinkle. He wants to remove our spotted garments that have caused us all our shame. Do you have on the wedding garment? Only the blood of the Lamb slain from the foundation of the world can clothe you in the righteousness of God (see 2 Cor. 5:21). Jesus paid quite a high price for you to be able to wear this beautiful garment. Don't try to appear before the King without it. It is the only garment accepted for salvation. You will need this to appear before the King, as well as before our enemy.

> *Now Joshua was clothed with filthy garments, and stood before the angel. And he answered and spake unto those that stood before him, saying, Take away the filthy garments from him. And unto him he said, Behold, I have caused thine iniquity to pass from thee, and I will clothe thee with change of raiment* (Zechariah 3:3-4).

Be Prepared

According to my dream, certain spiritual clothing is available for us today. The Lord wants us to put on the whole armor of God. He wants every person to be properly clothed so that all are ready for the days that we are about to enter.

Those who won't prepare now will not be ready for the coming harvest and the time of our Lord's return. They won't be able to handle the deception of the enemy as he comes to accuse. Their vessels will not be full of oil, and their lights will not be shining.

The Lord wants us to be properly outfitted for the journey He has set before us. Only with the clothes of His choosing and provision can we resist satan's onslaughts. Although Joseph wore a coat of many colors, this was usually given only to the firstborn son.

God is once again raising up dreamers and clothing them with His favor. He is not looking for a designer label or the name brand on our coats and shoes. Rather He is looking for those who will put on the garment He has specially prepared for us and who will produce the evidence of its fruit in our lives. He is looking for those who are clothed with the righteousness of Christ and whose feet are shod with the preparation of the gospel of peace.

Jesus said that we would know people by their fruit. Make absolutely certain that you have the fruit of the Spirit in your life and the proper coat for the journey. Without these, as manifested by the love of God and the humility of our Lord Jesus Christ (see Jude 20-23), you will suffer loss in the days ahead.

> *Every branch in Me that beareth not fruit He taketh away: and every branch that beareth fruit, He purgeth it, that it may bring forth more fruit* (John 15:2).

Ask the Holy Spirit to fill you with all His fullness and to help prepare you for the incredible journey that lies ahead. He has a garment for you to wear that He fashioned just for you, and He has already cleared out a path for you to walk on.

* * *

Lord, I desire to be clothed with the garment of righteousness and salvation and to be set free from my guilt and shame. Please remove from me, as You removed from Joshua, the filthy rags of my own works and religious motives and clothe me with the wedding garment You have adorned with Your favor (see Zech. 3:3-4).

Lord, I want to turn around and go Your way and not my own way. Holy Spirit, help me in my relationship with You. I don't want to just "take notes" all my life. I want to start to live for You and to fulfill my destiny.

Jesus, baptize me afresh and cause the fire of Pentecost to consume me as it did the early apostles. Lord, purge me so that I may bring forth more fruit in my life. I want to be ready to meet You and to be a witness. Clothe me with Your power and glory for the days ahead. Amen.

Chapter Four

One Hundred Fifty-Three Fish in the Sea of Humanity

Simon Peter went up, and drew the net to land full of great fishes, ***an hundred and fifty and three*** [153]: *and for all there were so many, yet was not the net broken* (John 21:11).

And Jesus said unto them, Come ye after Me, and I will make you to become ***fishers of men*** (Mark 1:17).

I believe that every true disciple of Jesus wants to learn how to "catch fish." Jesus promised His disciples that if they would follow Him, He would make them into fishermen. Regardless of his or her gift, every child of God can and should be a part of bringing in the harvest of "fish" that the Lord is bringing our way.

Many years ago, the Lord revealed to me that the Church in the last days would be like a net, gathering in fish of every kind (those of every nation, language, and tongue). Peter knew about these nets. Very likely every time he saw a fish, he was reminded of the Lord's words to him: "I will make you fishers of men." This might also be one of the reasons why the early Christians used a fish as a symbol for their gathering places. The number 153 in John 21:11 represents for me all the different kinds of fish (people) in the world. This number is also used meaningfully in the Old Testament.

> *And Solomon numbered all the strangers that were in the land of Israel, after the numbering wherewith David his father had numbered them; and they were found* ***an hundred and fifty thousand and three*** *thousand and six hundred* (2 Chronicles 2:17).

These people were foreigners from other lands who were numbered to build God's house. I believe that they represent those who will be caught up in Christ's net before His Second Coming.

After Christ had risen from the dead, Peter and the disciples went back to fishing. It says in John 21:3 that, once again, after fishing all night, they caught nothing.

Many of us have also been fishing all night long with little to show for all our great effort. On March 29, 1999, I was given a dream: I was standing beside two lakes fishing. There was a small bridge between the lakes. In my dream, there were no fish biting, and it was starting to get dark.

Suddenly, I found myself under the water looking at an empty hook dragging a rocky bottom. As I looked around I didn't see any fish. What I saw was the hook as it started to drift. As I watched, it traveled under the bridge and into the second lake, where I didn't see any fish either.

Next, I found myself standing on the bank of one of the lakes with nothing in my hand, not even a fishing pole. It was kind of depressing to just stand there. As I thought about my predicament, all of a sudden, a huge phone book appeared in my hands. By now I was standing next to what looked to be a river, and I found myself tossing the White Pages directory into the water.

Now to some, this may sound a little strange. I thought so, too. The next day I shared my dream at a pastors' conference in downtown St. Louis. When I arrived home that day, the new St. Louis White Pages directory was sitting by our front door. (It amazes me to think that God keeps such close tabs on your city and mine.)

I believe that the Lord was saying in this dream that fish need to be in the water before we can catch them, and that we need the right bait. We also need to make sure that we are fishing in the right locations, with nets, not just individual poles.

God can put an entire community in the river with just one toss (represented by the White Pages directory), but He won't do it until we are ready to bring them in. By the way, for those who are curious, yes I did go and toss the old one into the water just like in my dream. It was a prophetic gesture of what God wants to do in our city (see 2 Kings 13:18-19). And for all of you concerned conservationists, yes, I retrieved it afterward.

Ezekiel chapter 47 talks about the life-giving river of God. It describes the water as flowing from the right side of the temple. We need to be on the right side of the river if we're going to catch the fish we've been called to catch. We must go the way of the river. This is where the fish will be found.

> *And it shall come to pass, that every thing that liveth, which moveth, whithersoever the rivers shall come, shall live: and there shall be a very great multitude of fish, because these waters shall come thither: for they shall be healed; and* ***everything shall live whither the river cometh****. And it shall come to pass, that* ***the fishers shall stand*** *upon it from Engedi even unto Eneglaim; they shall be a place to spread* ***forth nets****; their fish shall be according to their kinds, as* ***the fish of the great sea, exceeding many*** (Ezekiel 47:9-10).

According to these verses, the Lord is once again calling for fishermen to stand by the river and spread out their nets. Several other dreams the Lord has given me also seem to relate to this message.

In the first dream, my wife and I were inside our home, but instead of being on land, our house was out on the sea. There were other houseboats, just like ours, all around. We were fishing, but instead of there being fish in the water, I saw people. Some were climbing up the side of our houseboat, while others were crying for help.

Many fish try to avoid getting caught, but when they recognize that there are sharks in the water or that some of the waters are becoming polluted and are no longer safe, they will jump in the net or boat any way they can.

God seems to be showing me that the water is like the sea of humanity. There are sharks out there, and the waters are getting more violent every day. If we are to fulfill God's purposes in these days, our home groups and churches must be places where people can come in and find rest and security from the raging waters of their lives.

A Sinking Ship

I was given another dream about the houseboats several years back, when my wife and I were in the process of starting a "Life Group" in our home. Thus it would seem that the Lord has been speaking to me, as well as to many other leaders and ministers, to start home groups or other forms of ministry so that our nets will be ready as the Lord starts to bring in the harvest. Luke 5:4-7 (TLB) gives us a clear picture of this:

> *When He had finished speaking, He said to Simon, "Now go out where it is deeper and let down your nets and you will catch a lot of fish!" "Sir," Simon replied, "we worked hard all last night and didn't catch a thing. But if You say so, we'll try again." And this time their nets were so full that they began to tear! A shout for help brought their partners in the other boat and soon both boats were filled with fish and on the verge of sinking.*

Many traditional churches today are just like the *Titanic* of years past. They are more concerned with maintaining their "unsinkable" image than with having enough boats that are capable of staying afloat during times of danger. We must make sure that we have enough "lifeboats" to carry to safety all the people who will run to us as the world waxes yet colder and as even our larger vessels begin to sink.

River Stages

Ezekiel 47:3-5 (TLB) gives a clear picture of what the Lord is about to do:

> *Measuring as He went, He took me 1,500 feet east along the stream and told me to go across. At that point the water was up to my* ***ankles****. He measured off another 1,500 feet and told me to cross again. This time the water was up to*

my ***knees****. Fifteen hundred feet after that it was up to my* ***waist****. Another 1,500 feet and it had become a river so deep I wouldn't be able to get across unless I were to* ***swim****. It was too deep to cross on foot.*

The outpouring of the Holy Spirit comes in stages. The "waters" rise first to the ankle, then to the knee, then to the waist. Finally, they flood over our heads and back again. These water levels are very significant, and the Lord wants each of us to experience each succeeding level. The water at our feet represents carrying the gospel. It wasn't until the priests' feet touched the water that the people were able to cross (see Josh. 3:14-16). Or, as is written in Romans 10:15a (TLB), "How beautiful are the feet of those who preach the Gospel of peace with God and bring glad tidings of good things."

Water up to our knees represents worship and lordship. Philippians 2:10-11 says that one day every knee will bow and every tongue will confess that Jesus Christ is Lord.

When the waters reach our waist, covering the reproductive area, we will see a level of outpouring that will bring forth many new births. This is also the point at which new dreams will be born and entire ministries will come forth. The waist is also related to truth and balance, as Paul said in Ephesians 6:14:

Stand therefore, having your ***loins*** [waist] *girt about with truth, and having on the breastplate of righteousness.*

The water over our heads will cause the gospel to go out to the entire world. At this level we must learn how to swim in the river of God, letting go of our man-made ideas and philosophies, being fully yielded to the Holy Spirit, and allowing Him to flow forth from our lives.

Fishing While the Sun Is Up

Our nets (churches, home groups) need to be ready for all the different types of fish the Lord will soon be sending our way. Many people have heard about the success of David Yonggi Cho's ministry in South Korea. All I can say is that with multiple thousands of home groups, he must be doing something right.

While many have been called to go to the nations, we need to recognize that the nations are also living right here among us. Some of us are being called as "welcomers" to welcome new believers here into the family of God. Over 20,000 people are anticipated to immigrate to the United States this year from Kosovo alone. Churches with home groups offer a wonderful opportunity for people from all cultures to be an active part of the local church, while still reaching out to those in their own communities who are most like them. Home groups can also help eliminate the loss of identity felt by those of other cultures as they enter a Western congregation and are struggling with possible cultural differences.

There must be some sort of contact point within each local church for people from other nations as they come to Christ. This is probably the largest overlooked area in the Body of Christ with regard to the "harvest." Churches need to seek faithful leaders from each people group to lead home groups that can reach out to those who speak their own language or share a common cultural identity.

Why should those of other nations who have recently come to Christ have to go back into the world to find help? I'm not saying that I know how to do all this, and personally, I do not feel equipped for the task, but I still see the need. God sent Jethro to Moses to show him how to designate certain leaders for certain tasks. This model has continued to be very effective in the Church from the early days even into our own time.

I am sharing all this here because of a very powerful dream that the Lord gave me. The events in this dream were so real that I actually thought it was taking place. I found myself walking with a group of people whom I didn't know, when all of a sudden, I saw fish up in the sky, reaching from one end of the horizon to the other. There must have been at least a thousand fish, and I could see each one clearly. Although there were other things in the dream, it is the fish that I want to focus on.

Only the Lord could have orchestrated such a fabulous display. Each fish moved along in place up in the sky above me. About one-half of the people in my group looked up and saw the same thing. However, not everyone in the group was able to see this vision. The others kept looking up and then down again, wondering what the rest of us were looking at.

This dream was so real that I began to praise God. As I raised my hands toward Heaven, thanking God for His goodness to the children of men, I closed my eyes and started thanking Him for saving me and for allowing me to see such an awesome sight.

All of a sudden, I started to feel heat all over me. In my dream, I opened my eyes and saw that the sun had risen up above me. It was so beautiful–like nothing I'd ever seen before. In the natural, you can't look at the sun very long without hurting your eyes, but this was different. It was a breathtaking experience to simply stare at the sun without having to turn away. I could feel its heat and watch it rising in all its splendor and beauty.

This dream was given while I was asleep on the couch in my front room. When I woke up, I was completely intoxicated with the presence of God. It felt as though I was completely under water. I could feel the Spirit's presence from the top of my head to the bottom of my feet. *Apparently, the risen sun had caused the healing waters of the Spirit to rise.* This is what happened to the lame man in the third chapter of Acts.

> *And he took him by the right hand, and lifted him up: and immediately his feet and ankle bones received strength. And he leaping up stood, and walked, and entered with them into the temple,* ***walking****, and* ***leaping****, and* ***praising*** *God* (Acts 3:7-8).
>
> *"But for you who revere My name, the* ***sun of righteousness will rise*** *with healing in its wings. And* ***you will go out and leap*** *like calves released from the stall. Then you will trample down the wicked; they will be ashes under the soles of your feet on the day when I do these things," says the Lord Almighty* (Malachi 4:2-3 NIV).

People all over the world need healing and restoration. As we lift up our Lord, He will draw all men to Himself. The Son has risen and is the light of the world for all who are willing to see. Jesus said in Matthew 5:45 that God causes the sun to rise on the good and the evil, and that He makes His rain to fall on the just and the unjust. Let the Son shine upon you. Then get ready for the latter rain of His Spirit, which He is pouring out to bring new life and resurrection power. Allow Him to revive and refresh you once again.

Safe in His Hands

The final dream related to this subject occurred while I was in India. I was taking a night train from Madras to Madurai with a group from my church in St. Louis. Our itinerary for the next day was to visit the Meenakshi temple, a leper colony, and a small Indian village. That night on the train I had a dream about beautiful fish of all different colors swimming in the water. Suddenly, I saw two cupped hands go down into the water. Instead of seeing the fish swim away as I expected, they all swam into those hands.

According to *Numbers in Scripture*[1], the words *fishes, the net*, and *joint heirs*, as well as the expressions *sons of God* and *creation of God*, are all related to the number *153*.

Thus this number represents all the different kinds of people who will be caught up in the *gospel net*. They will become the *joint heirs* of Christ and will be the true sons of God who make up the creation of God, that is, those who are born of His Spirit. The 153 fish also seem to represent the children whom God has numbered and who have been destined to build His house (see 1 Kings 5:15; 2 Chron. 2:17-18).

I shared my dream about the multi-colored fish the next day in a little village in southern India. The people there were very open and responsive. They gathered around our entire team afterward. Just like in the dream, their hearts ran to God. God wants to gather the fish from every nation into His hands. His love is drawing multitudes to Him from India and from other countries around the world.

Before I left for India, I was given a vision in which I actually saw India from above. Then I saw the country being lifted up as though an invisible hand was picking it up from its left side. I then saw the entire country being turned into a book, with the pages being flipped backward on the left side. Each page, as well as the cover, retained the exact

1. E.W. Bullinger, *Numbers in Scripture* (Grand Rapids: Kregel Publications, 1967), 275-276.

shape of India. I believe that God was saying that India's history has yet to be written. Even as God has a destiny for every person, so He also has one for every country and people group.

When portions of this book were still in the beginning stages, it was translated into the Hindi language of India. I was somewhat taken aback by the response and the hunger of the people of India who requested copies of it. In only a few months, it sold many thousands. It has also been selling well in England and in Russia. This simply demonstrates that people all over the world want the "good news." They are just waiting for someone to bring it to them. The Lord has allowed all nations to walk after their own ways, but now He commands all nations to repent and return to Him (see Acts 17:30).

After I had returned from India, my wife met a lady named *Niranjana* and I met a man named *Sukhvinderjit.* The woman's name means "light comes up in the darkness," and the man's name means "happiness after much struggle." I later found out that the *Meenakshi* temple in Madurai, which I visited, is named after the goddess Meenakshi, which means "one with fish-shaped eyes." In their tradition, it is believed that this goddess protects her children by gazing at them with her eyes. This is supposed to stir up spiritual life in those who worship her.

In contrast to this Hindu belief, I believe that our Creator, the God and Father of our Lord Jesus Christ, now has His eyes upon His children in India. He wants to protect them, stir them up, and take them out of darkness and into the light of the gospel of Jesus Christ. This will end their struggle to be reunited with their Creator, which in turn, will give them true happiness and the only way to everlasting peace.

Today the Lord is not only telling the people of India to run back to Him and swim into His hands where it is safe, but He is also speaking to each one of us in every nation to start seeking His hand. Isaiah 55:6 tells us to seek the Lord while we can still find Him and to call upon Him while He is still near. Since He is now near, we need to seek Him with our whole heart. Who knows how long He will be able to be found?

> *Behold, the days come, saith the Lord God, that I will send a famine in the land, not a famine of bread, nor a thirst for water, but of hearing the words of the Lord: And they shall wander from sea to sea, and from the north even to the east, they shall run to and fro to seek the word of the Lord, and shall not find it* (Amos 8:11-12).

Put God's Word on your line and get ready to throw out your life preservers. Let down your nets. There are at least 153 large fish (countries, nations, and tribes) waiting to be made free at last, and some will be coming through the doors of your home and your church. Are you ready to do some fishing?

Look up and open your eyes! He is "gazing" upon you even now. The fish are all around you waiting to be safely held in His hands! Once we all are in His hands, He will then lift us up to see His face, and we will see the fire of love in His eyes.

> *Be silent, and know that I am God!* ***I will be honored by every nation. I will be honored throughout the world*** (Psalm 46:10 NLT).

> *I will bring them also to My holy mountain of Jerusalem, and make them full of joy within My House of Prayer. I will accept their sacrifices and offerings, for My Temple shall be called "A House of Prayer for All People"! For the Lord God*

> *who brings back the outcasts of Israel says,* ***I will bring others too besides My people Israel*** (Isaiah 56:7-8 TLB).

> *I have other sheep, too, in another fold. I must bring them also, and they will heed My voice; and there will be one flock with one Shepherd* (John 10:16 TLB).

> *His name shall endure for ever: His name shall be continued as long as the sun: and men shall be blessed in Him: all nations shall call Him blessed* (Psalm 72:17).

* * *

Jesus, help us to become "fishers of men." Teach us, like You have taught many others, to see not only our little world but also Your heart for all people everywhere. Open our eyes to see those around us who are hungry to know You. Cause Your Son to rise upon us and to bring the rain of Your Spirit down upon us that we may live again.

Cause us to see the harvest of fish that is all around us, and cause Your light to begin to heal and restore us so that we can be vessels in Your hand to do the same for others. Lord, place us in the right waters so that when You come, we can once again be in Your hand, and You can take us up to be with You forever. Amen.

Chapter Five

A Candle in the Dark

He will not break the bruised reed, nor quench the dimly burning flame. He will encourage the fainthearted, *those tempted to despair. He will see full justice given to all who have been wronged. He won't be satisfied until truth and righteousness prevail throughout the earth,* ***nor until even distant lands beyond the seas have put their trust in Him*** (Isaiah 42:3-4 TLB).

For Thou wilt **light my candle***: the Lord my God will enlighten my darkness* (Psalm 18:28).

The spirit of man is the candle of the Lord (Proverbs 20:27a).

I the Lord have called you to demonstrate My righteousness. I will guard and support you, for I have given you to My people as the personal confirmation of My covenant with them. You shall also be a light to guide the nations unto Me (Isaiah 42:6 TLB).

For the earth shall be filled with the knowledge of the glory of the Lord, ***as the waters cover the sea*** (Habakkuk 2:14).

Looking at some of the events in our world, it seems that darkness is closing in all around us. Wars, famines, and other sorrows are causing hope to fade from view. It's easy to feel that our little light can't really make much of a difference in a world steeped in so much darkness.

One night, I had a dream in which I heard no words. It was as though I was watching a movie in that I was able to view what was going on around me. The scene in my dream was at night, and I could see the sea in the background.

All of a sudden, a candle, which was sticking out of the sand, came into focus. What was unusual was that this candle was bent over, and its wick was just barely lit. It seemed to barely make a dent in all the darkness surrounding it. Since I could feel the wind around me, I thought that the candle couldn't possibly stay lit with such a strong breeze.

As I continued to stare at the scene before me, I began to hear a gurgling or bubbling that seemed like it was coming from below the surface of the sand. Pretty soon bubbles started to form all around the base of the candle. The candle continued to remain at a slant, and the wick didn't get any brighter, but I noticed that water started to flow out from around the candle's base. The water continued to get deeper until it flowed out in all directions, as though it was heading toward the sea, where it would mix together as one body of water.

The Lord Lifts the Fallen

Please note that God didn't raise the candle in my dream to stand up tall or to cause its flame to grow brighter. Instead, He showed that life-giving water could still flow out of it, even though it didn't look as if it could produce much.

I have felt like this candle many times. I'm sure you have too.

As long as the light of the gospel shines forth, there is still hope for the nations. Our light may sometimes seem to be dim, but if we allow the wind of the Spirit to blow new life into us, I believe that we can rise again. As you read this, say to yourself: *I may not be much, but greater is He who is in me than he who is in the world* (see 1 Jn. 4:4). *I can do all things through Christ who strengthens me* (see Phil. 4:13). *With You, Lord, all things are possible* (see Mt. 19:26).

God takes those who are bowed down and makes them sit with kings. Psalm 145:14-16 (TLB) says:

> *The Lord lifts the fallen and those bent beneath their loads. The eyes of all mankind look up to You for help; You give them their food as they need it. You constantly satisfy the hunger and thirst of every living thing.*

Let us allow His abundant goodness to pour forth from our lives so that our lights may shine and others may see our good works and glorify our Father in Heaven (see Mt. 5:16). Let us be those candles. We might look a little bent over, but let's stand tall despite the winds of adversity that try to stop us from becoming all God meant for us to be. Let us allow the winds of the Holy Spirit to ignite our fire once again and to refresh and renew us so that we can give His light and power to those who still sit in darkness.

> *Arise, My people! Let your light shine for all the nations to see! For the glory of the Lord is streaming from you. Darkness as black as night shall cover all the peoples of the earth, but the glory of the Lord will shine from you* (Isaiah 60:1-2 TLB).

One With the Sea

People everywhere have the same needs. Every one of us came into this world as a bent candle. We are all in need of love, joy, peace, forgiveness, healing, and a sense of belonging. Not one of us is perfect now, and in this life, we cannot hope to be. Our needs cannot be satisfied with that which is bought. Only through the shed blood of Jesus can we hope for wholeness. This is why Jesus wants every person from India to China, Russia to England, Iraq to Israel, Africa to Japan, and Australia to the uttermost parts of the earth, to have the light of the gospel shine upon them.

Jesus said that this telling of the gospel in all places would be the true sign to herald in the end of this age (see Mt. 24:14). If all of us "bent candles" would get together, our combined light would shine so bright that all the nations would come to know Christ as the true light that shines in the darkness. Fire is fire. It doesn't matter how big or bright it is. Just one spark can set an entire forest aflame.

As the Body of Christ, we need to stop comparing our "wattage" with one other. What matters is that we all let our lights shine. Christ taught that words can take down mountains (see Mt. 21:21), and mustard seeds can grow into huge trees (see Mt. 13:31-32). He also demonstrated that a few fish can be multiplied to feed thousands (see Mt. 14:19-21). Christ's light can't be extinguished no matter how dim some may believe it to be. This is because His light is eternal.

I picture the candle in my dream as Christ's light in an individual. Through His Body (the Church), this light can reach the nations with the life-giving waters of the gospel. The end result will be the outpouring of the Holy Spirit upon all flesh, as prophesied in Joel. In my dream, the waters poured out in all directions from the candle's base and became one with the sea. The waters seem to represent the outpouring of the Holy Spirit, and the sea represents all the nations of the world.

> ***When the poor and needy seek water,*** *and there is none, and their tongue faileth for thirst,* ***I the Lord will hear them,*** *I the God of Israel will not forsake them. I will open rivers in high places, and fountains in the midst of the valleys:* ***I will make the wilderness a pool of water,*** *and the dry land springs of water* (Isaiah 41:17-18).
>
> *And He saith unto me,* ***The waters*** *which thou sawest, where the whore sitteth,* ***are peoples, and multitudes, and nations, and tongues*** (Revelation 17:15).

According to Isaiah 2:2, the mountains of the Lord's house will be established over the top of all other hills and all nations will flow toward it. Someday, Christ's Kingdom will extend across all boundaries, and all people groups of the world will come to Him.

> *After this I saw a vast crowd, too great to count,* ***from every nation and tribe and people and language,*** *standing in front of the throne and before the Lamb. They were clothed in white and held palm branches in their hands* (Revelation 7:9 NLT).

The glorious "good news" is that Christ died on the cross, was buried, and rose again the third day for you and for me (see 1 Cor. 15:3-4). Jesus wants all people to hear and accept this good news. So strong is His passion to see this that He showed me in a dream one time a person who had never walked with Him even one day of his life. Then He told me that He would be willing to go back to the cross and repay the price He had paid so that this one individual could be in Heaven with Him.

What kind of love is this? This is the love that we all need and can't live without. Christ's new resurrected life can be born anew in each person who accepts Him. The gospel is the "good news" that sin's debt has been paid by the only One who could pay it.

John the Baptist said of Christ in John 1:29b, "Behold the Lamb of God, which taketh away the sin of the world." Jesus is the light in the darkness; this is the message of hope for all nations that you and I are called to proclaim. "Christ in you" is the "hope of glory" (see Col. 1:27).

The Son has truly risen and His new life can be yours! His resurrection life can be the light of every man who has ever come into this world. Do you see why satan wants to stop this message from getting out? This revelation will end his rule over your life once and for all. Hallelujah!

* * *

Jesus, help me share the "good news" with people everywhere, be they people from overseas or those in my own community. Help me to be that candle, Lord. I know that my light can be dim at times, but let Your light shine through me so that people may know the love You have for them. Lord, help me to encourage those who don't know You yet, by letting them know that You truly are the Light of the world. Amen.

Chapter Six

The Rising of the Sun

A New Song

On February 3, 1996, while I was lying on my bed praying in the Spirit, I was given a song in the middle of the night. Now this wasn't just an inspiration; I actually heard the song being sung to me while I was awake. Whether it was given to me by the Holy Spirit or by angels, I don't really know. All I know is that I actually heard this with my own two ears, and that it came from Heaven. These were the words that were sung to me:

> "The rising of the sun and the rising of the sea,
> The rising of the sun and the rising of the sea."

These words were sung to me twice. Why the Lord chose to do this for me and not someone else, I'm still not sure. I do believe that the song was sung twice so that I would remember the words exactly as they were given, but also to emphasize that certain things are getting ready to come to pass sooner than we think. In Genesis 41:32 (TLB), we can gain some understanding of this:

> *The double dream gives double impact, showing that what I have told you* ***is certainly going to happen****, for God has decreed it, and it is going to happen soon.*

The next day I looked up each use of the phrase "the rising of the sun" in my Bible. It is interesting to note that *the first time* this expression is used is in Numbers 2:3, and that this song was given to me on February 3, 1996 (2/3/96). Also, in the previous Chapter, I mentioned the number *153*. The first time that number is used is in First Kings 5:15. Again, it was on May 15, 1995 (5/15/95) that the Lord spoke to me regarding it. I've recorded more details regarding His words to me concerning this in Chapter Ten.

Also, a lady named Beverly Neidorf was given a similar revelation in February of 1996, the same month and year I was given this song. This is what she wrote in the 1998 Spring issue of the *Morning Star Journal*[1]:

> "Long after David's Tabernacle was no longer standing, Amos prophesied of a day when God would raise it up again (Amos 9:11). In February 1996, the Lord spoke to me that he was extending the key of David's house to his psalmists. In Isaiah 22:22, we find reference to the 'key' that will once again unlock the door for intimate spontaneous worship of the Lord."

The Scriptures say that every word should be established in the mouth of two or three witnesses (see Mt. 18:16). At the same time the Lord was giving me this song, He was

1. *Morning Star Journal*, Vol. 8, #3, 60.

also confirming this word to another one of His children in the Body of Christ.

The tribe of Judah was the first tribe mentioned in the order God gave to Moses as to how Israel should travel in the desert. *Judah* means "praise." Thus "praise" was to lead God's people–the other tribes–through the wilderness. Even during the reign of Jehoshaphat, the singers and worshipers led the way to victory in battle against the enemies of the Lord (see 2 Chron. 20).

Praise is to lead the way. Why? Psalm 22:3 tells us that God inhabits the praises of His people. As the singers led the way with singing and praise to the Lord, Israel's enemies began fighting among themselves.

The Scriptures also reveal in other places that music is a mighty weapon. It was the anointed music from David's harp, for example, that delivered Saul from his depression (see 1 Sam. 16:23).

When my wife plays her harp, the peace of God just reigns. She has been playing for only about two years, but the Lord has already been anointing her music. Praising the Lord brings the Holy Spirit's presence upon the congregation, and the Lord displaces the presence of evil with Himself. This causes His enemies to be scattered. Jesus said in John 12:32:

> *And I, if I be lifted up from the earth, will draw all men unto Me.*

Isaiah 42:10 (TLB) says:

> ***Sing a new song to the Lord;*** *sing His praises, all you who live in earth's remotest corners!* ***Sing, O sea!*** *Sing, all you who live* ***in distant lands beyond the sea!***

As we begin to praise the Lord and lift Him up, His power begins to flow as a river. In God's time, this mighty, flowing river will affect people from every nation, tribe, and tongue, and they too will join in the chorus. The rise of anointed music in the midst of His people is an undeniable affirmation confirming what God wants to do. *God wants a new song to be sung to the nations.*

God is also getting ready to join each member of His Body from these many people groups until we all become one. When we come together in unity, this will fulfill Christ's prayer in John 17:21:

> *That they all may be one; as Thou, Father, art in Me, and I in Thee, that they also may be one in Us: that the world may believe that Thou hast sent Me.*

This is what will cause the world to believe. As we enter the new millennium, each of us needs to ask the Lord what our part should be in taking the gospel to the nations. This is crucial because world evangelism will not happen without prayer. Prayer needs to be sent up to the throne of God by the people of God, asking that His mercy would be shown to the people and leaders of all nations. We have a responsibility to intercede for the whole world.

> *I exhort therefore, that, first of all, supplications,* ***prayers****, intercessions, and giving of thanks, be made for all men; for kings, and* ***for all that are in authority****; that we may lead a quiet and peaceable life in all godliness and honesty. For this is good and acceptable in the sight of God our Saviour;* ***who will have all men to be saved****, and to come unto the knowledge of the truth. For there is one God, and one mediator between God and men, the man Christ Jesus; who gave Himself a ransom for all, to be testified in due time* (1 Timothy 2:1-6).

> *Then saith He unto His disciples, The harvest truly is plenteous, but the labourers are few; pray ye therefore the Lord of the* ***harvest, that He will send forth labourers into His harvest*** (Matthew 9:37-38).

Supporting the Laborers

There are many ministries the Lord has ordained for this task of bringing all people everywhere the "good news." I'll just mention a handful of them that are bearing obvious fruit.

The first I would like to mention is the "Jesus Film" project. This film on the life of Jesus is sponsored by Campus Crusade for Christ. It has been translated into nearly 500 different languages thus far, and about 200 more translations are slated to be done. This film has been seen by over one billion people. And according to official ministry statistics, in the first quarter of 1999, more than 800 different mission organizations, churches, and denominations have joined into partnership with this one ministry alone, reaching across almost every country of the world.

Paul Eshleman, who is currently the director for the "Jesus Film" project at Campus Crusade for Christ, shared this story in one of their ministry newsletters. In Bihar, India, a Hindu girl died and was taken to the place of the dead. While she was there, she was instructed by the Lord that she would be allowed to live on earth for another seven days as a witness that Jesus was the only way to Heaven. For the next seven days, she traveled with a Jesus Film crew, testifying to people the way of salvation. After seven days, she died again, just as she said she would. This is just one example of how the Lord is speaking to all nations regarding their need of Him. I want to encourage you to watch it yourself on the Internet at www.jesusfilm.org.

God wants all of us to start letting down our nets for the harvest and to financially support and pray for those who are taking His Word across the world. Let us join with the angels in singing His song. Romans 10:14-15 (TLB) says:

> *But how shall they ask Him to save them unless they believe in Him? And how can they believe in Him if they have never heard about Him? And how can they hear about Him unless someone tells them? And how will anyone go and tell them unless someone sends him? That is what the Scriptures are talking about when they say, "How beautiful are the feet of those who preach the Gospel of peace with God and bring glad tiding of good things." In other words, how welcome are those who come preaching God's Good News!*

Let us sing a new song to all nations. The Lord is coming soon! Let us prepare our hearts for Him to enter in and carry the gospel to the ends of the earth. The Son has already risen! The sea will be rising again! May we be candles that are shining the light of the glory of God to the nations.

> *And nations shall come to Your light, and kings to the brightness of Your rising* (Isaiah 60:3 AMP).

> *I am the Lord, and there is no other; apart from Me there is no God.* ***I will strengthen you, though you have not acknowledged Me,*** *so that from the* ***rising of the sun*** *to the place of its setting men may know there is none besides Me. I am the Lord, and there is no other* (Isaiah 45:5-6 NIV).

> *From the* ***rising of the sun*** *unto the going down of the same the Lord's name is to be praised* (Psalm 113:3).

> *And* **this gospel** *of the kingdom shall be preached in all the world for a* ***witness unto all nations;*** *and then shall the end come* (Matthew 24:14).

After the Lord spoke to me in the night, my wife and I wrote the following song:

"The rising of the sun and the rising of the sea;
There's a cry in each and every heart, that's longing to be free;
They all need to feel His love; He's reaching out to you and me.
(chorus)
On the cross He saved us. Through His blood we're freed from sin.
By His love He's healed us; with new life we're born again.
No more chains to bind them; no more walls to hold them in.
Let all nations praise Him; let all nations rise to Him.
The rising of the sun and the rising of the sea;
Jesus said, 'If I be lifted up, I'll draw all men to Me.'
Let all nations praise His name, across each shore from sea to sea."

* * *

Father, I pray that You would put a new song in our hearts. May it be a song of praise unto You, our God. I pray that You would use us to impact people of other nations. Help us to reach out and welcome those who have come to our shores from other lands—both here in the U.S. and abroad. Help us to be like Isaiah who said, "Here am I; send me" (Is. 6:8). Give us Your heart for the nations. Help us to see our part in bringing the gospel to the whole world.

Cause us to prosper so that we may support those who are already being used to share Christ with the nations, and help us bring Your healing love to all those who have never heard. Amen.

Chapter Seven

You Are Worth More Than Gold

How the gold has lost its luster! Even the finest gold has become dull. The sacred gemstones lie scattered in the streets! See how the precious children of Jerusalem, ***worth their weight in gold****, are now treated like pots of clay. ... The people who once ate only the richest foods now beg in the streets for anything they can get. Those who once lived in palaces now search the garbage pits for food* (Lamentations 4:1-2,5 NLT).

Restore us, O Lord, and bring us back to You again! ***Give us back the joys we once had!*** *Or have You utterly rejected us? Are You angry with us still?* (Lamentations 5:21-22 NLT)

I looked on my right hand, and beheld, but there was no man that would know me: refuge failed me; ***no man cared for my soul*** (Psalm 142:4).

And the publican, standing afar off, would not lift up so much as his eyes unto heaven, but smote upon his breast, saying, ***God be merciful to me a sinner*** (Luke 18:13).

I know that many people all over the world feel like they are not worth very much. Untold numbers of people struggle at some point in their lives with low self-esteem, frustration, and feelings of helplessness. I'm sure that those in Kosovo and other war-torn countries, in particular, have been feeling a great sense of hopelessness and despair. Many are full of fear and doubt, while others feel lost and wonder if they'll ever be found. Many are insecure in their relationships with others as well as with God. These beleaguered souls feel like they've been left as a dull gemstone that has been discarded upon the highway of life. Many wonder if they will ever see the light of day again.

We know inside of us that there is something more, but we also feel a sense of desperation–that our lives can't make a difference or that our hopes and dreams can never be fulfilled. The sun seems to always shine on others–but not on us.

Many of us feel worn out and used up. We wonder if God even knows that we're here or if He cares about us at all. It seems that peace and joy have faded from many shores. From the White House to our schools, bloodshed and violence have become all too common. In a number of nations around the world, persecution against Christians has increased dramatically and has left a dark stain upon those lands. Many people are now asking, "Is there any hope left for me? Does anyone even care?"

Shining His Light

Well, I believe that God wants to show us how we can obtain that inner peace and assurance of His love. He is shining His light to make us new again. He sends the "Son's" rays to give light to even the smallest object. Jesus wants to be the light of our lives, and He will be, if we will only ask Him to be.

We are worth much more to God than our weight in gold. He compares us to precious gemstones that sometimes may be scattered in the streets. When I was in India, I saw many people who had lost their sense of self-worth. *God wants people of every nation to know that there is Someone who cares about them.* Jesus cared enough about us to lay down His life for us. He lived a perfect life without sin to pay the debt created by our own sin. No one else born to humanity has ever lived an entirely sinless life. No one else ever could. If we would each get honest for just one moment, we would see that Christ's death on the cross was the only possible payment for the penalty that we all deserve.

> *For all have sinned, and come short of the glory of God; being justified freely by His grace through the redemption that is in Christ Jesus* (Romans 3:23-24).

Jesus bought us at a great price. We are valuable and precious to Him. According to the Word of God, we're worth more than all the combined wealth of this world. Jesus asked a question in Mark 8:36-37. He said:

> *For what shall it profit a man, if he shall gain the whole world, and lose his own soul? Or what shall a man give in exchange for his soul?*

The Missing Watch

One human soul is worth more than all the riches of the earth. I would like to attempt to illustrate this truth for you by sharing a dream I was given.

In my dream, I found myself driving down a highway, when all of a sudden, the sun's rays lighted upon a small object that had been abandoned at the side of the road. It looked like something that was made of gold. I turned my wrist to look at my watch, hoping to see that I had time to go back and find out what the object was. To my surprise, my watch was missing from my wrist.

At this point in the dream, I need to give you a little background information: I wear a gold watch on my wrist all the time. There is an alarm on it, so I also wear it to bed. It is very special to me because it was my dad's, and it reminds me of him.

When I first tried to put it on, I noticed that the band was broken and it didn't keep time anymore. Apparently, my dad hadn't worn it in quite some time as it had also lost all its luster. Thinking that it would never work again, I almost pitched it. After all, it really had no value except the sentimental value it had for me.

On the inside of my dad's watch are inscribed these words: "The Captain." In Hebrews 2:10, Jesus is called "the captain" of our salvation. Today this watch is very special to me because it reminds me of my relationship with Jesus and my relationship with my dad, who has gone on to be with Jesus. Dad's watch (even though it has little monetary value) is therefore absolutely priceless to me.

When I realized in my dream that my watch was missing, I thought that maybe the gold object near the side of the road might be my watch, so I made a U-turn and went back to where I thought I had seen it. As I was driving back, I saw a man come out of his house and walk toward the location where I had seen the sun lighting upon the gold object.

At this point I decided that if I didn't do something quick, I'd never see my watch again. While speeding up, I watched the man arrive at the location where I had first seen the gold object. He leaned over, picked up something, and then started to head back to his house. I honked my horn, but he didn't turn around.

In the dream, I drove right across the median and up onto the man's lawn. He looked a little surprised because I almost ran over him. I could see that the gold object was still in his hand. I rolled down my window and told him that I thought what he had in his hand was mine.

When he opened his hand, I saw that it was my gold watch. So I asked him to check the engraving on the inside. He looked and sure enough, the words "The Captain" were engraved upon it. Upon seeing this, he handed me my watch.

The moment it touched my hand, a thought came to me. The man himself was like the gold watch. God considers him to be much more precious than gold. He might be broken on the inside and dull on the outside, but if someone would just wipe away the dust and let the light of the Son of Man shine upon him, we would see real gold there. I then asked the man if he had ever received Christ into His life and quoted to him this Scripture from John 1:12b (TLB):

> *But to all who received Him, He gave the right to become children of God. All they needed to do was to trust Him to save them.*

I told the man who had picked up my watch that he didn't have the right to be called a child of God unless he received Jesus as his Lord and Savior. I also told him that the Lord wanted him to live in Heaven with Him; that this was why Jesus had to die on the cross; and that there was just no other way to be saved. It says in Acts 4:12 (TLB):

> *There is salvation in no one else! Under all heaven there is no other name for men to call upon to save them.*

Recovered Jewels

As I thought about my dream, God clearly revealed to me that the reason I turned around and went back was because my watch was special to me. I was willing to turn around on the highway, speed up, honk my horn, cross over the median, and even drive up on this man's lawn to retrieve something that was mine.

I want you to consider the following questions: How important is God to you? How important to you is His will and His plan for your life? What are you willing to do to discover your destiny and to find your way back to God? Have you misplaced or lost your Father's gift? If you have, you need to go back and get it or it could be gone forever. Jesus is reaching out His nail-scarred hands to you right now while you are reading this book.

You can't buy your salvation or do anything to earn it. Salvation is God's free gift. All He requires of you is that you acknowledge your need of Him and your inability to make it on your own without His help. Calling on the name of the Lord is like placing your empty hand in His and saying to Him, "Only You can save me. I've tried to do it myself and have failed every time. None of my religious training has given me any joy or peace. I am now at the place in my life where I acknowledge that You alone are Lord, and it is only through Your shed blood and Your resurrection life that I can be made whole."

Just as I turned around on the highway to retrieve what was mine, Jesus came from Heaven to this earth to get back what was His. We were made for Him. He loves us and wants us to have a relationship with Him that will last throughout eternity. He lived on this old earth for over 33 years proclaiming God's message of love, healing, and forgiveness to all who would hear.

He chose to go to the cross willingly for you and for me. He suffered more than any man has ever suffered to redeem us from the enemy of our souls. This is how important we are to Him. Just as I honked to get the man's attention, Jesus is now proclaiming His message loud and clear throughout His Church. He wants to get your attention before He comes again to take His family home to be with Him.

Has your watch stopped ticking? Does it need to be rewound? David said in Psalm 31:15, "My times are in Thy hand...." According to Ephesians 5:16, we are to redeem the time because the days are evil. Is your time running out? According to Second Peter 3:9 (NIV), God is not "slow in keeping His promise, as some understand slowness. He is patient with you, not wanting anyone to perish, but everyone to come to repentance."

Sometimes He will even have one of His children "drive up on your lawn" to get your attention. If you don't mind, I'm going to park my car on your lawn for a moment so that I can ask you some questions: Do you know that Jesus loves you? Have you ever been born again, asking Him to forgive you of your sins? Have you received Him into your life as your Lord and Savior and publicly told another that Christ has saved you? Have you been baptized, showing the world, as well as the rest of God's family, that your relationship with Jesus is real? Are you presently walking with the Lord and living as though you're loved and embraced by Him, or are you still living in darkness and going your own way?

A tree is known by the fruit it bears. Jesus said in John 8:12:

> *Then spake Jesus again unto them, saying,* ***I am the light of the world: he that followeth Me shall not walk in darkness,*** *but shall have the light of life.*

You can be a child of God by truly giving your whole life to Him. For all that you or I know, *this may be the last message you will ever hear during your lifetime.* So I'm trying to get your attention now–even if I offend you while I am parked on your lawn–so that I know that I did my best to tell you. It is better to end up in Heaven having been slightly offended than to end up in hell having never accepted the truth.

Pure Gold

Remember, you are worth much more to God than gold. He has done everything He can to save you from death and destruction. Christ already paid your debt on the cross, and He offers you complete forgiveness and a relationship with Him. Receive Him now! Confess Him as your Lord and Savior. Romans 10:9-10 tells us that if we confess Jesus as Lord with our mouth and believe in our heart that God has raised Him from the dead, we will be saved; and in Romans 10:13 it says that if anyone will call upon the name of the Lord, he will be saved. Call out to Him, and He will save you.

When we confess Him before men, He will confess our name before the Father (see Mt. 10:32). Likewise, if we deny Him before men, He will also deny us (see 2 Tim. 2:12).

Stop right now! Do you really want to go to Heaven? Do you have on the wedding garment that I mentioned in Chapter Three? Are you sure that if you died right now, you would spend eternity with the King of kings and Lord of lords and be part of His glorious homecoming celebration?

Or would you be cast into outer darkness? Do you want to be cleaned up and made into pure gold?

If you haven't accepted Jesus as your Lord and Savior, put down this book and don't go any farther until you have asked Him to save you. Don't be like the man who chose not to wear the garment that the King had provided for him. If you truly want Him to save you, He promises that He will answer you if you call upon His name now.

I encourage you to pray the following simple prayer. I also encourage you to pray afterward from your own heart and in your own words. Ask the Holy Spirit to direct your words to Him. Pour out your heart to Him. Let the Holy Spirit draw you even now as you yield your life to the Lord Jesus in this moment that is between only you and Him. *Remember, your eternity is at stake here. Where you will spend it is based solely on your relationship with Him.*

Prayer

> *Dear Lord Jesus, thank You for dying on the cross for me and for shedding Your blood. I know that I am a sinner, and I know there is nothing I can do to earn Your forgiveness. I come empty-handed with nothing to offer You. Lord, I need You today. Have mercy upon me, O God. I repent of my sin. I want to be born again and to be accepted as Your child.*
>
> *I surrender my whole life to You. I want to live for You. I want to be able to honestly call You my Friend, as well as my Savior and my Lord. I desire to turn away from all known sin in my life, and I ask You to make Your home inside of me forever. Please save me from eternal judgment and help me learn to walk with You.*
>
> *Lord, please don't leave me on this earth when You come for Your Bride. I know that You could return this*

very hour. Thank You for not leaving me behind. Help me to begin now to know You intimately and to be used in Your Kingdom as a powerful instrument to help others come to know You. I say yes to You and to Your plan for my life. Help me to find my destiny.

I ask You now to write my name in the Lamb's Book of Life. I want to serve You with my whole heart all the rest of my days. I want to have You say to me in that day, "Well done, thou good and faithful servant. Enter into the joy of the Lord." Help me to share Your love with those You've placed around me. Open my eyes so that I may come to love my brothers and sisters as members of Your family.

I desire even now to confess You before men as my Lord and Savior, and I believe in my heart Your Word that says if I call upon Your name with an honest and sincere heart, You will save me. Father, I call upon You now to save me in Jesus' name. Amen.

Make this prayer your true heart's cry. If you are real with God, He will be real with you. I would like to be the one to personally assure you of your salvation, but only the Holy Spirit can do that. The Scriptures say that only the Holy Spirit can bear witness with our spirit that we truly have become the children of God.

I also want to warn you that Jesus said that many would come to Him in that day saying, "Lord! Lord!" but would not enter Heaven. He is not looking for lip service here on earth, but for a sincere heart that really wants a vital relationship with Him. Christ's Lordship will show up in your life if you yield to Him. His love will be evident in you because if God is truly your Father, you will become like Him. An apple tree produces apples, and a thorn tree produces thorns.

The Lord is seeking for pure gold–gold refined by the fire of His presence. Job 23:10 shows how our lives can be refined as gold under the Refiner's touch: "But He knoweth the way that I take: when He hath tried me, I shall come forth as gold."

God wants to renew you once again. He yearns to dust you off, shine you up, and put you back in the place you were always meant to be–with Him forever.

> *...You are to live clean, innocent lives as children of God in a dark world full of people who are crooked and stubborn. Shine out among them like beacon lights, holding out to them the Word of Life* (Philippians 2:15-16a TLB).

Matthew 22:9 reveals our new vocation as sons and daughters of the King. We are to "go...therefore into the highways, and as many as [we] shall find, bid to the marriage." And we can be assured of His faithfulness to save us in the end.

> *Then they that feared the Lord spake often one to another: and the Lord hearkened, and heard it, and a book of remembrance was written before Him for them that feared the Lord, and that thought upon His name. And they shall be mine, saith the Lord of hosts,* ***in that day when I make up My jewels****; and I will spare them, as a man spareth his own son that serveth him. Then shall ye return, and discern between the righteous and the wicked, between him that serveth God and him that serveth Him not* (Malachi 3:16-18).

It is our heavenly Father's will that all the gold of the earth be reclaimed. Let's bring in the gold to fill the Father's house, and let's allow the Son of His presence to shine His light on us and through us once again.

* * *

Jesus, help me see those around me that You are shining Your light upon. Give me more boldness to share the glorious good news of salvation with those I come across every day. Be the Captain of my salvation and help me live out my Christian faith.

Help me to recover that which I have lost and to find out what You have planned for my life. I desire to not just call You "Lord" with words alone, but also with my deeds and actions. Help me to proclaim Your Lordship over my life to those around me.

I now confess You as my Lord and Savior, and I am looking forward to the day when I will stand before You clothed in Your righteousness and beholding You in all Your glory. Thank You, Jesus, for giving me the right to be called a child of God. I thank You that Heaven has now become my future and eternal home. Amen.

Chapter Eight

From Fear to Freedom to Fellowship

And deliver them who through ***fear*** *of death were all their lifetime subject to bondage* (Hebrews 2:15).

For ye have not received the spirit of bondage again to fear; but ye have received the Spirit of adoption, whereby we cry, Abba, Father (Romans 8:15).

The fear of man *bringeth a snare: but whoso putteth his trust in the Lord shall be safe* (Proverbs 29:25).

Now the Lord is that Spirit: and where the Spirit of the Lord is, there is liberty (2 Corinthians 3:17).

Those of you who prayed for salvation while reading the last chapter now have the hope of eternal life, and I want to be the first one to welcome you into the family of God. I also want to exhort you that if you are not involved in a local church or body of believers, you need to start seeking the Lord so that you can find your place. If you are a new Christian or one who has just returned to the Lord, there will be many obstacles you will need to face to become all that God has called you to be. This chapter deals with certain areas that we all need to confront.

Each of us has at least one area of weakness we were born with that we can learn to overcome only with Jesus' help in our lives. Now that you have chosen to truly follow Jesus, many issues will begin to rise to the surface in your life. This next dream I would like to share greatly influenced me and helped me to overcome some of these areas in me. It helped me to set a new direction in life.

In this dream, I found myself in downtown St. Louis, and the city looked like a war zone. I stood between two brick buildings that had no windows. I could hear bombs exploding all around me, and I could see men, women, and children hiding in bunkers. I heard gunshots and what sounded like machine-gun fire.

As a Christian, I was doing my best to share Christ with people, but I was afraid of getting killed; and it was obvious to me that my witness was not bearing much fruit. For some reason, I ended up hiding behind a telephone pole, pondering the idea of just keeping quiet about my faith and trying to think of a way to make it out of the city alive. How I thought that hiding behind a pole would keep me alive, I don't know. I guess being as thin as I am does have some advantages.

While I was still hiding, a man came up beside me with a grenade in his hand. He was planning to throw it at one of the two buildings. At this moment, I was confronted with a choice. If I said nothing, many innocent people would die. If I spoke up, I might be killed. I was put into a situation that required me to make a quick decision: *Would I let fear rule my life so that I said nothing, or would I obey God and speak up?* My decision would mean life or death for some.

Well, at that exact moment, the Spirit of God must have risen up inside of me because I suddenly started to boldly confront the man. I told him that he had better count the cost before he carried out his wicked deed or he would burn in hell for eternity. I knew it wasn't just my voice, but that I was being aided by the Spirit of God.

I remember that the man just stood there and stared at me. Then he stared at the implement of destruction in his hand. In no time at all, he fell down on his knees, crying and pleading for God to forgive him for what he was about to do and asking God to save him.

It's a Mystery

As I was standing beside the man with the grenade, I noticed another man much like myself who was standing nearby. We were about the same height, but his hair was longer than mine was. He was talking to people and asking them to receive the Lord. I started following him around, trying to remain unnoticed. It seemed that he had no fear and knew exactly what he was doing, and I felt very inadequate compared to him.

As it came toward evening, he made his way to a small path away from the battle. Instantly, we were in an area with beautiful homes, lush green lawns, and flowing streams. There was no sound of war, just a quiet sense of peace and security.

I came up behind him and said, "Sir, excuse me! I was following you as you shared the gospel in the city, and I just want to know how you can to be so confident and sure of yourself." He answered me saying, "It's the *mystery*!" Some other things occurred in the dream as well, but I want to focus on this "mystery" that he spoke about.

At the time when this dream was given, I was dealing with some major issues in my life with Sue, as well as with my stepson, Josh. I was feeling "dry" in my Christian walk and couldn't quite find where I fit. I knew that there was more to this new life than I was experiencing, and I saw many areas in my life where I still needed to get free.

According to my dream, I was in a spiritual battle that encompassed not only my family, but other areas of my life as well. I had to make the choice whether I would allow fear or other unpleasant circumstances to keep me from growing in my faith, or whether I would seek some help and direction from another brother who was apparently walking in greater liberty than I was.

These choices in life are not uncommon. What we choose can affect many, as was true in my dream. Fear always prevents us from becoming all that God has called us to be. The "mystery" the man spoke about is what Paul wrote about in Colossians 1:27. The "riches of the glory of this mystery" is "Christ in you, the hope of glory."

Paul said, "...I no longer live, but Christ lives in me. The life I live in the body, I live by faith in the Son of God, who loved me and gave Himself for me" (Gal. 2:20 NIV).

God Never Meant for Us to Do It Alone

For many years, I didn't understand the full implications of this "mystery" the man spoke to me about in my dream. Just recently, however, the Lord gave me the interpretation. In my dream, I was all alone trying to share the gospel in my city. The mystery that Paul wrote about can only be accomplished as we come together. Jesus said in Matthew 18:19-20:

> *Again I say unto you, That if two of you shall agree on earth as touching any thing that they shall ask, it shall be done for them of My father which is in heaven. For where two or three are gathered together in My name, there am I in the midst of them.*

If Christ is not in our midst, our witness will have little effect. This is why He sent His disciples out by twos, never alone. I used to be part of a group that thought we could do it all on our own without the help of our brothers and sisters. We were going to "reach the world" with the Word. Well, we learned the hard way that our greatest obstacle wasn't the devil, but the Lord Himself.

God knows that we can't do it on our own, so He will stop any group with a spirit of pride that declares they can "do it" without Him or the rest of His Body. God never meant it to be just *my church* or *your church* that will touch our cities. It's the collective vision and work of the entire Body of Christ that will get the job done.

You know that you are in the wrong group if you believe that you and your church are the only ones who will reach the world. As long as you have this mindset, you are destined to fail. Criticizing another man's vision won't cause yours to succeed. In fact, God will make sure that your vision does not succeed because He will not allow any flesh to glory in His presence. God will do it His way and not ours because His way is the only way that will work. It will be your vision and my vision bonded together in love that will make the puzzle or "mystery" complete.

Don't Let Fear Stop You

> *For God hath not given us the spirit of fear; but of power, and of love, and of a sound mind* (2 Timothy 1:7).

We all must make the choice to confront our fears. If we don't, those fears will try to overcome us and to stop us from doing God's will. We should not allow fear to stop us from God's call on our life. King David said in Psalm 34:4 that he sought the Lord and that the Lord delivered him from all his fears. Only the power of the Holy Spirit can eradicate fear. Fear is one of the greatest forms of bondage from satan that you can have, and it is the anointing of God that destroys this yoke.

Once I was sharing the gospel downtown near the Darst Webbe projects in St. Louis. After witnessing in one area, I moved to another area. Suddenly I stopped because I couldn't believe my eyes. I found myself standing in between two brick buildings without windows, and believe it or not, they were identical to the ones in my dream. There I was sharing the gospel of Christ without fear in the very place in which I had been hiding in my dream. God took me from "fear to freedom to fellowship." This time I wasn't alone.

Fear always tries to stop us from becoming all that God has called us to be. However, God continues to call us, just as He called Gideon even though he was hiding from the Midianites (see Judg. 6:11). Even the disciples were hidden behind closed doors because of fear (see Jn. 20:19). The Lord taught Joyce Meyers, who has an international ministry to both women and men, a lesson about this a few years ago. He told her that when she was afraid to do something, to just "do it afraid."

We all have to deal with fears and insecurities in our lives. However, we must each remember that we are not alone. This is what the mystery is all about. Several of our brothers and sisters are still working on these same issues in their lives. Even though Gideon was hiding from the Midianites, the angel still called him "a mighty man of valour." God sees us differently than man does. He sees the inside of us, the inner man of the heart.

One of the greatest mysteries I see is how God continues to use us in spite of our failures. I want to exhort you to go ahead and challenge those fears. If what you want to do is for the glory of God, go for it! There is a great mystery at work here. Christ is in you, and He is your hope of glory. What an awesome mystery–knowing that He who is in you is greater than he who is in the world.

> *To the intent that now unto the principalities and powers in heavenly places might be known by the church the manifold wisdom of God, according to the eternal purpose which He purposed in Christ Jesus our Lord* (Ephesians 3:10-11).

> *Herein is our love made perfect, that* ***we may have boldness*** *in the day of judgment: because as He is, so are we in this world.* ***There is no fear in love; but perfect love casteth out fear****: because fear hath torment. He that feareth is not made perfect in love. We love Him, because He first loved us* (1 John 4:17-19).

> *And he answered,* ***Fear not: for they that be with us are more than they that be with them*** (2 Kings 6:16).

* * *

Father, I don't want anything to hold me back from sharing Your love. I pray that You would deliver me from all my fears. Holy Spirit, anoint me with Your boldness to take a stand for what is right. Strengthen me so that I will never cower in the presence of evil.

Cause me to see that greater is He who is in me than he who is in the world (see 1 Jn. 4:4). Jesus, cause me to triumph over all my enemies. Help me work together with the rest of Your family to set those free whom satan has bound so that they too can experience the joy and freedom that is found in You alone and in the fellowship of Your family. Amen.

Chapter Nine

The Anointed Generation

Let no man despise thy youth; but be thou an example of the believers, in word, in conversation, in charity, in spirit, in faith, in purity (1 Timothy 4:12).

I could write an entire book about the topic of this particular chapter, even though I have felt somewhat out of touch with the world of teenagers. I sometimes feel very inadequate talking about their world because I haven't been able to keep up with all the fads and styles of this new generation of teens. Yet the Lord has given my wife and me a heart for these young people, and I know from experience that the word we speak can have a lasting effect upon them.

The Light of Life

One day during my senior year at Kirkwood High School, I was smoking marijuana out in the smoking area with some friends of mine. As soon as the pipe reached me, it went out. Since none of us had a light, the group volunteered me to go to another group and get a lighter or some matches. I noticed a tall, young man talking to a group of teenagers. I walked up to the group and asked them if anyone had a light. This man turned to me, looked me right in the eyes, and said, "I have the light of your life, Jesus Christ!"

My wife and I used to have a radio program called "Let Your Light Shine." I named it this because of the words that were spoken to me by that young man back in my high school. When he spoke those words to me, my mind went back to my earlier days at Sunday school and how time and again I had tried to follow this Jesus of Nazareth.

Yet I had begun doing drugs and living for the world's pleasure. I was lost and lonely when this man pointed it out. His words affected me greatly. Acting as if I hadn't heard him, I returned to my friends with some matches. But I still remember his words today: "I have the light of your life, Jesus Christ!" I really wanted what that man had, but I didn't believe that I was worthy of it.

As a teenager, I basically gave up on almost everything. I saw no purpose in school other than to just get through it. I was having major communication problems with my family, and I had very low self-esteem. Since I was doing drugs at the time, I was also living with paranoia and fear. To put it lightly, I was pretty confused. Whatever light I once had thought I had wasn't able to overcome all the darkness.

Even though I had begun thinking that my new lifestyle was cool, the road I was going down was leading me to depression, loss of identity, and isolation from those who cared about me. I felt alienated from others as well as from God. When I didn't have money for drugs, I would find whatever I could to produce the same high. I used all types of prescription drugs, and I would sniff glue or whatever substances I could find. I also became hooked on pornography.

Sometime after this man told me that Jesus could be the light of my life, God delivered me from a very bad situation that could have had terrible consequences. I promised God then that if He would cover for me this one last time, I would start seeking Him. After that I really began to have a hunger to know Him better. When I finally turned my life over to Him, Jesus delivered me from alcohol, drugs, and many other bondages that had become part of my life.

I still remember the day, as though it were yesterday, when I gave my life to the One who wanted to be the light of my life. I stood in church during the altar call, and I knew that the Holy Spirit had His hand on my heart. I knew that He was telling me to go forward and commit the rest of my life into the hands of my Lord.

The Lord has also brought my wife through many things. Sue married young after dropping out of college. She quickly found herself divorced, alone, and a single mother with a troubled son, living in great poverty. I remember that day in a little Baptist church in Eureka, Missouri, where she also recommitted her life to the Lord. To this day, neither of us has any desire to return to our old lives.

After all those years in darkness, I can now honestly and without reservation tell any teenager who is involved in drugs or any other bondage that Jesus is the only way out of that darkness. Ask Him, and He will become the light of your life, too.

I implore you to begin to seek God and other people who can help you so that you can begin to step out of the darkness and into the light. Jesus will hold your hand and be your best friend. He will help you because He really loves you and wants you to be delivered even more than you do.

I've had several dreams from the Lord about teenagers and the struggles they go through. The first one I would like to share involved a teenager in our church.

What Are You Carrying in Your Back Pocket?

The dream opened with me walking out of my house. Following close behind me was a particular teenager. In the dream, he was my own son, living in my house, and he was getting ready to go out for the night. I was in a good mood, and he looked like he was too.

I reached out my arm and patted him on the back like a buddy, but my hand bumped against something in his back pocket. His shirttail was out, and it covered whatever the object was. I grabbed the object out of His pocket and found out that he was carrying a gun. I yelled, "What do you think you're doing? You could get yourself killed!" I then woke up.

Acts of teenage violence in the past few years in Texas, Kentucky, Oregon, Colorado, and Georgia show that this has become a very real problem among our youth. Teen violence is now considered by many to be one of the greatest problems in our society. In fact, the most recent shootings by the two teens in Littleton, Colorado, show how serious this problem really is.

Every teen needs a vision for his or her life. They need to be able to find their purpose and have dreams. They need to see that their lives matter to our Lord and that they have a destiny to fulfill. One of the two boys responsible for the killings in Colorado was overheard saying in the midst of the wicked deed, "This is what I always dreamed of doing."

How tragic! Whatever happened to the boy who dreamed of being a firefighter or the girl who desired to help others and become a nurse when she was grown? Granted, there are many young people who dream and accomplish wonderful things for the Lord and for others, but there are still many who live without dreams or a purpose for their lives.

Just after the Littleton tragedy, the news media aired a news clip to show that the youths may have been trying to re-enact a recent movie that depicted a similar scene with gunmen wearing long trench coats and shooting as they moved down a corridor. The movie showed the same type of trench coats that the boys were wearing at the time of the murder. Yet it was later revealed that one boy had been planning this massacre for over a year.

Could this type of violence and tragedy be the result of taking prayer out of our schools? Movie makers had better beware of the types of movies they are producing. Movie makers and lawmakers alike will have to answer to God some day and give an account for what they have produced.

I believe that the Lord was showing me through my dream how important it is to know what is going on in your teenager's life. Parenting is not all fun and games. Many of our youth are dealing with matters of life and death. Shirttails and trench coats may cover up what is on the outside, but many of these teens are dying on the inside and are in desperate need of answers.

A short time after my dream, I saw the mother of the young man I had seen. I told her about the dream. She informed me that her son had begun hanging around with a gang and he had just been in a fight where a juvenile had pulled out a gun. After sharing my dream with the youth, I was able to counsel with him. I shared with him Second Corinthians 10:3-6 (TLB):

> *It is true that I am an ordinary, weak human being, but I don't use human plans and methods to win my battles. I use God's mighty weapons, not those made by men, to knock down the devil's strongholds. These weapons can break down every proud argument against God and every wall that can be built to keep men from finding Him. With these weapons I can capture rebels and bring them back to God, and change them into men whose hearts' desire is obedience to Christ. I will use these weapons against every rebel who remains after I have first used them on you yourselves, and you surrender to Christ.*

I warned the young man that he could be killed. I also told him that God has a plan for his life, a plan that didn't include death in some alley. I prayed for him and exhorted him to spend much time in God's Word. At last report, this young man had become involved with a group called Teen Challenge, which helps young people get away from gangs and drugs.

I thank God for Teen Challenge and other ministries that have risen up to help troubled youth get right with God and get their lives on the right track again. God's family is the only gang that anyone should be involved with, and the only weapon our youth should be taking up is the sword of the Spirit, which is the Word of God. In fact, Scripture talks about putting on the whole armor of God so that we can stand in these desperate times:

> *Last of all I want to remind you that your strength must come from the Lord's mighty power within you. Put on all of God's armor so that you will be able to stand safe*

> *against all strategies and tricks of Satan. For we are not fighting against people made of flesh and blood, but against persons without bodies–the evil rulers of the unseen world, those mighty satanic beings and great evil princes of darkness who rule this world; and against huge numbers of wicked spirits in the spirit world. So use every piece of God's armor to resist the enemy whenever he attacks, and when it is all over, you will still be standing up* (Ephesians 6:10-13 TLB).

Get Out Fast and Don't Look Back

If you are going to stand for God, you must leave the past behind.

> *No, dear friends, I am still not all I should be, but I am focusing all my energies on this one thing: Forgetting the past and looking forward to what lies ahead, I strain to reach the end of the race and receive the prize for which God, through Christ Jesus, is calling us up to heaven* (Philippians 3:13-14 NLT).

What in your past is holding you back? Let it go! What are you carrying in your back pocket? Get rid of it! Is it worth dying for? Walk away from your past and leave it behind. Ask the Lord to help you forgive anyone who has wronged you; this includes your parents, friends, and society in general. Do whatever you need to do to get things right again. He will heal you of past resentments if you'll let Him. First Peter 5:7 says to cast all your care upon Him because He cares for you.

God can be awesome in your life! The future is yours, and it's up to you to decide what you'll do with it. Teens, get as far away from drugs as you can. Stay away from those who are involved with them before it is too late.

In another dream, I found myself between two houses. A friend of mine, whom I hadn't seen since I was a teenager, was telling me that he too had left the drug scene and become a born-again Christian. I was excited for him, but then I saw him pull out a cigarette and light it. As we continued to talk, his words caused me to really question whether he was saved or not.

Before long, we were both entering the back door of a house. In my dream it was the house on the left. I noticed that people were doing drugs downstairs, and many were standing up smoking marijuana. Others looked as though they were shooting up other forms of drugs. Still others were just sitting around doing nothing. My friend started to walk toward a group of teens who were passing around drugs, when all of a sudden, everyone began to faint and fall down.

I sensed something very evil and told my friend that we needed to get out of there quickly. He kept delaying, so I finally ended up having to leave without him. As I was exiting through the back door, almost everyone in the room was down on the floor. Some were holding their stomachs and groaning. Others looked dead. I ran out of there as fast as I could and didn't look back.

Young person, you may be standing between two houses right now. The children of Israel found themselves with a similar choice.

> *I call heaven and earth to record this day against you, that I have set before you life and death, blessing and cursing: therefore choose life, that both thou and thy seed may live: that thou mayest love the Lord thy God, and that thou mayest obey His voice, and that thou mayest cleave unto Him: for He is thy life, and the length of thy days: that*

> *thou mayest dwell in the land which the Lord sware unto thy fathers, to Abraham, to Isaac, and to Jacob, to give them* (Deuteronomy 30:19-20).

To "choose life," we must turn our backs and run from sin. Most of the teens today have no idea of the danger they are in. Sometimes their entire futures are at stake. Just one bad choice can cause years in jail, total isolation from family and friends, and the loss of future opportunities for a fulfilling adult life. I want to exhort any teen reading this book, as well as every parent, to flee from sin. *Get that thing out of your back pocket before it is too late!*

> *Brethren, if any of you do err from the truth, and one convert him; let him know, that he which converteth the sinner from the error of his way shall save a soul from death, and shall hide a multitude of sins* (James 5:19-20).

We have been given only one life to live, to witness, and to serve our Lord Jesus Christ. Don't you understand that God sees and knows about everything? Don't try to hide things from God. He knows what your "shirt" is covering. The only thing you should be hiding is God's commandments in your heart. The Lord instructs youths to do just that.

> *Wherewithal shall a young man cleanse his way? by taking heed thereto according to Thy word. With my whole heart have I sought Thee: O let me not wander from Thy commandments. Thy word have I hid in mine heart, that I might not sin against Thee* (Psalm 119:9-11).

Don't play with sin. One thing can lead to another quicker than you think.

> *Then when lust hath conceived, it bringeth forth sin: and sin, when it is finished, bringeth forth death* (James 1:15).

Harmless or Deadly

Some people do drugs and use the excuse that since God put the plants on earth, why not partake of them? It is interesting to note that the Greek word for "witchcraft" is *pharmakai*, from which we get our word *pharmacy*. I believe that the Lord puts drug abuse in the same category as witchcraft. God also equates witchcraft with rebellion and idolatry (see 1 Sam. 15:23). Rebellion, witchcraft, idolatry, and drugs are not good in any combination. If you mix them together, they add up to death and hell.

Come to the Light if you really want to get your life right with God. Just because something looks harmless doesn't mean it is. A good example of this is a snake. Some snakes are harmless. Others are poisonous. Just because God made the snake doesn't mean that all snakes can be handled the same way. I've learned this with my two pet snakes, a sand boa and a boa constrictor. (Indiana Jones still refuses our invitations to come to our house.)

I had a dream one time that had a snake in it. Now, I have been around snakes long enough to recognize which are poisonous and which are harmless. The snake I saw in my dream was a harmless one. But as it turned its head, I noticed a little black spot that moved when it did. I then recognized that a poisonous black spider was on a web attached to the snake. The snake wasn't a problem to me; but the spider that came along with it was.

The very next day as I was driving on a side road next to our church, a black snake was crossing the road at the same time. Although most people run when they see snakes, I don't. I stopped my van and jumped out to catch it. However, I soon realized that I had nothing with me in which to carry the snake home.

Looking around I found a bag on the side of the road. I looked inside it to see if there were any holes in it. As I did, I noticed a spider in the bag. Then I remembered the dream I had had the night before. I left the bag behind and let the snake go.

The Lord taught me an awesome lesson with this. Some things that you allow in your life may seem harmless at first, but we must still beware because it's the "little foxes" that can spoil the vine. Be aware of what might come along with it. *Do you really know what is in the bag? Your bag could be "laced" with death!* Most teens who are hooked on drugs, alcohol, or pornography probably thought a little smoke here, a little taste there, and a little look there would not be a problem. Those who are now hooked probably wish they had never started.

Our pastor has said that we each need to draw the line somewhere as to what we will allow and what will not allow in our lives. Because they wouldn't set clear boundaries and eventually made the wrong choices, many now live in prisons. They probably wish that they could turn back the clock of time and begin again.

Surrender your life to the Lord. Do it now, teenager, while there is still time! Beware of what you have been allowing into your life. There is a "destroying angel" out there seeking whom he may devour. Pray so that you may have the strength to overcome these youthful temptations that are coming your way. Submit to God and humble yourself, and the devil will have to flee (see 1 Pet. 5:5-9).

Just look at what God did with King David when he was a youth. Anything is possible with God. God is once again calling out the "Davids." Be a young man or a young woman after God's own heart. You can be an example to other teens of how Jesus can be the Light of their lives too.

Come forth and take your place as God's ambassadors. You've been hidden for a while, but now is the time for you to awake and arise. The enemy has been saying all along that he is your friend, but he is a liar, and his real motivation has been to destroy you. Rise up young men and women of God. Leave the past behind you and reach out to the One who "sticks closer than a brother" (see Prov. 18:24).

* * *

Lord Jesus, help our teenagers to become examples to others of Your work in their lives. Show them that You are their only real Friend and reveal to them the emptiness and dissatisfaction of life without You. Help them to become the anointed generation You've called them to be. Jesus, be the light of their lives so that they can see their way out of the darkness that tries to blind them from seeing Your direction in their lives.

Lord, speak to them through Your Word, through Your servants, and through dreams and visions of the night. Reveal to them Your will concerning the purpose and destiny that You have designed and planned for their lives. Holy Spirit, be to them Counselor, Teacher, Comforter, and most of all, True Friend.

Lord, help us as parents to believe in our teenagers and to see them as You see them. Help us train them up in the way they should go so that they will not depart from the course You have set for their lives. Amen.

Chapter Ten

The Effect of Every Vision

> *And the word of the Lord came unto me, saying, Son of man, what is that proverb that ye have in the land of Israel, saying, The days are prolonged, and every vision faileth?* (Ezekiel 12:21-22)

> *...and the word of the Lord was precious in those days; there was no open vision* (1 Samuel 3:1).

> *Where there is no vision, the people perish...* (Proverbs 29:18).

On May 15, 1995, I was praying in my basement. As I was deep in prayer, a very strong anointing came upon me. I could tell that something very unusual was about to take place. I told the Lord that if there was something He wanted to get through to me, I was willing to receive it; but to be honest with you, I didn't expect what came next.

The anointing of the Holy Spirit began to increase upon me until I became more aware of the spiritual realm than of the natural. Yet I was still physically awake and still conscious of my surroundings. I then heard these words being spoken to me. I could hear them just as though someone was speaking to me. My wife was asleep next to me, so I can't say that they would have been audible to anyone else, but they were certainly audible to me.

At the time these words were given I was awake and sitting up in my bed. Here are the words I heard: "*The effect of every vision shall be retained no longer.*"

I had never heard these words before in my life, I assure you. I also had never experienced a vision while I was awake. Yet at the same moment these words were spoken to me, I was able to see a man standing in front of me who looked like he was from a foreign country. In my vision, I saw that his eyes were closed. When he opened them, I could see that he was blind. It looked as though there was something over his eyes.

In the vision, I then saw hands being laid upon him and I saw his eyes open. As I continued to sit up in my bed, the Holy Spirit's presence remained strong for what seemed to be about an hour. It was absolutely an awesome experience.

I continued to sense the Holy Spirit's presence when I awoke the next morning. This lasted for about three hours, although not with the same intensity as I had felt the night before. The next day I took out my computer Bible and typed in the words *effect* and *vision*. Never had I heard or seen this phrase before, but right before my eyes there it was, "the effect of every vision." There is only one place in Scripture where these two words are used together. It is found in Ezekiel 12:23:

> *Tell them therefore, Thus saith the Lord God; I will make this proverb to cease, and they shall no more use it as a proverb in Israel; but say unto them, The days are at hand, and* ***the effect of every vision.***

During a time of Israel's rebellion, Ezekiel received words to tell his own people that some incredible things were about to occur:

> *The word of the Lord also came unto me, saying, Son of man, thou dwellest in the midst of a rebellious house, which have eyes to see, and see not; they have ears to hear, and hear not: for they are a rebellious house* (Ezekiel 12:1-2).

Some of the things Ezekiel said didn't sound as though they could happen as suddenly as the prophet claimed. However, some of the people believed his words. Others thought that what he said would only happen in some far-off distant future. Yet the prophet was claiming that the things the Lord had spoken would come to pass in their lifetime. I believe that the Lord is getting ready to do some incredible things, and He wants all of us to get ready and to be prepared to be a part of what He is about to do.

The day after I was given these ten words, I got out a Webster's Dictionary (Ottenheimer Publishers, 1958) and looked up the word *effect*. It means "the impact or fulfillment of a cause." Other definitions are, "to become operative" and "the bringing to pass of a desired result." A vision can be a prophetic dream or revelation. It is most often referred to as that which can't be seen by the natural eye.

The word *retain* means "to continue to keep in possession of." Now, if you put this all together, you could say: *Every prophetic, redemptive revelation or desired result that can't be presently seen with the natural eye shall become operative or shall be brought to pass with a great impact and will be kept in possession no longer.* In other words: *All kinds of things are getting ready to "break loose."* I believe that this can apply to an individual, a church, or the entire Body of Christ.

I suggest that every person who is reading this book look up every usage of the words *effect*, *vision*, and *retain*. These words came from Heaven. *If you believe nothing else in this book, believe these words, for they will be fulfilled at their appointed time.*

A *vision* will produce a strong desire placed in your heart by God. It will be a desire to do something that will lead others to Christ, and it will glorify Him. I believe that the fulfillment of both will begin to have a major impact upon the Church of Jesus Christ and upon our world.

I believe that the Lord has retained certain things for a time, but He is now removing certain previously held restraints. Science tells us that for every cause, there is an effect. This is also true in the spiritual realm and includes every redemptive revelation and purpose of God. Not only does this relate to God's promises but also to His judgments, since we will reap whatever we have sown–whether it is bad or good. God sees the end from the beginning, and He can reveal any part of His redemptive plan to anyone at any place or time.

> *So repent (change your mind and purpose); turn around and return [to God],* ***that your sins may be erased*** *(blotted out, wiped clean), that times of refreshing (of recovering from the effects of heat, of reviving with fresh air) may come from the presence of the Lord; and that He may send [to you] the Christ (the Messiah), Who before was designated and* ***appointed*** *for you–even Jesus, whom heaven must receive [and* ***retain]*** ***until the time for the complete restoration of all that God spoke*** *by the mouth of all His holy prophets for ages past [from the most ancient time in the memory of man]* (Acts 3:19-21 AMP).

There is a restoration of all things getting ready to take place. I don't know when the final fulfillment of this will be, but I do know that He is beginning to reveal His truth to us as never before. He wants to open our eyes and show us His plan that He ordained before the world began. He is not only opening the windows of Heaven and pouring out His Spirit upon all mankind during this time of refreshing, but He is also allowing many judgments to fall in various places upon this earth.

If we want to change the "effects" that we have been experiencing, we also need to make sure that we are supporting the right "causes." Tornadoes, earthquakes, floods, and fires are judgments because of the evil that is being sown in our land. We need to repent of our godlessness. Jesus has been standing at the door of many homes, churches, and nations, and some have been saying no to Him and yes to satan. What will it take for us to learn that *we will reap what we sow*?

Anyone who has eyes to see can observe that our world is rapidly changing around us. Even the earth itself is registering the effects of man's rebellion against our Lord. It is groaning for the day that it too shall be delivered from this corruption.

> *For I reckon that the sufferings of this present time are not worthy to be compared with the glory which shall be revealed in us. For the earnest expectation of the creature waiteth for the manifestation of the sons of God. For the creature was made subject to vanity, not willingly, but by reason of Him who hath subjected the same in hope, because the creature itself also shall be delivered from the bondage of corruption into the glorious liberty of the children of God* (Romans 8:18-21).

I believe that the Lord is getting ready to unveil or reveal many of His hidden purposes. Matthew 10:26 says that there is nothing covered that will not be revealed, and nothing hidden that will not be made known. Deuteronomy 29:29 says there are certain secrets that the Lord keeps to Himself, but what He reveals to us is to help us understand His laws. Even Daniel was told to "seal the book" until the time of the end. He said that many would "run to and fro" and that knowledge would increase toward the end of time (see Dan. 12:4).

Not only is this sudden increase of knowledge an indicator of the times in which we live, but if we read Matthew 24:32-34, we will better understand the role Israel is about to play. I was given a dream on November 19, 1997, in which I saw Jewish rabbis coming to faith in the Messiah after seeing the broken foundation stones–upon which the disciples of Jesus walked–uncovered after almost 2,000 years and completely restored whole again before their very eyes. I will share this dream in *Dreams in the Spirit Volume II.*

An Appointed Time

Three days later, on May 18, 1995, the Lord spoke to me again by His Spirit. This time I wasn't even praying. I was actually wrestling on the floor with my wife and my son Daniel. I think this makes quite a statement concerning what God thinks about our time spent with our families. Here I was wrestling with my son, and the Lord was still able to speak with me. (He obviously considers my family time very important.) Maybe He also, in a sense, was wrestling with me as He wrestled with Jacob. Could it be that He was trying to get the message across that He also is a Father like me, and that He too likes to spend quality time with his family and enjoys wrestling with His kids?

These next words came without my feeling any anointing at all. Just like the song in Chapter Six, they were given to me twice.

"The vision is for an appointed time.
The vision is for an appointed time."

After I heard these words, I typed the words *vision* and *appointed* into my computer Bible, and once again, there is only one place where these two words are used together. I found these words in Habakkuk 2:1-3:

> *I will stand upon my watch, and set me upon the tower, and will watch to see what He will say unto me, and what I shall answer when I am reproved. And the Lord answered me, and said,* ***Write the vision****, and make it plain upon tables,* ***that he may run that readeth it. For the vision is yet for an appointed time****, but at the end it shall speak, and not lie: though it tarry, wait for it; because* ***it will surely come****, it will not tarry.*

According to these verses, there is a set time when that which is not seen will become manifest. I've decided not to interpret these two words any further but to let the Word of God stand by itself. Jesus said in Acts 1:7 that the times and seasons are in the Father's hands. I believe that it is imperative, therefore, that I leave them there and not try to determine something I'm not meant to know.

However, I do know that *God is up to something big*, and I want to be a part of it. This is one reason I wrote this book. But how about you? Have you started to become involved in what God is doing today? I hope so. If not, please let me encourage you to get involved and to take your place in God's great plan and purpose of the ages. God wants you on His "dream team."

Time to Wake Up and Open Our Eyes

It is now time to wake up and start walking out our calling. We are not to walk blindly, unaware of our Master's plans. Rather we are to understand fully where He is taking us and what He wants us to do. The army that God is raising up will be able to hear what the Spirit is saying and will follow Jesus, their Commander and Chief. *The fulfillment of every vision is ready to come to pass.* Let's go forward and take the land. *This is our appointed time.* Let us open our eyes to see our individual part in God's vision. Let's do mighty exploits for our God.

> *...Go ye into all the world, and preach the gospel to every creature* (Mark 16:15).
>
> *Also I heard the voice of the Lord, saying, Whom shall I send, and who will go for Us? Then said I, Here am I; send me. And He said, Go, and tell this people...* (Isaiah 6:8-9).

* * *

Lord, open our eyes to see that the times and the seasons are in Your hands. May we be like the sons of Issachar, who had an understanding of what You were up to in the earth. May we be the ones who will see the impact of every prophetic revelation and be involved in the fulfillment of Your plan for all ages. Cause us to once again dream Your dreams so that we may fulfill our God-given destiny. Amen.

Chapter Eleven

Never Give Up on Your Dreams

God believes in you and has a wonderful plan for your life!

> *...I am come that they might have life, and that they might have it more abundantly* (John 10:10).
>
> *For I know the plans I have for you, says the Lord,* ***They are plans for good and not for evil****, to give you a future and a hope* (Jeremiah 29:11 TLB).
>
> *And it shall come to pass in the last days, saith God, I will pour out of My Spirit upon all flesh: and your sons and your daughters shall prophesy, and your young men shall see visions, and your old men shall dream dreams* (Acts 2:17).

Many people have given up on many of their God-given dreams. In some cases it is for fear of the problems that may occur due to computer chips failing in the year 2000. Although I agree we must all prepare for possible hard times ahead, I don't agree that we should abandon all our plans and make this our main focus. My purpose here is not to share about Y2K, but to look beyond the year 2000.

What we sow into the Kingdom of God will multiply itself–not only in the "here and now" but also in the "there and then." I would suggest that all who read this before the next millennium go and talk with a pastor or go to a local Christian bookstore and read about proper ways to prepare for Y2K. (Of course, if you're reading this after the year 2000, then you already know how the story has turned out.)

Since this sort of thing has never happened before, none of us can really claim that we have all the answers. Still, I believe that it would be very careless to do nothing to prepare yourself. On the other hand, building an underground bomb shelter would be overdoing it a bit. Be encouraged, even after the "smoke" clears, there will still be "life" after the year 2000. There are still many books to be written, songs to be sung, words to be spoken, and people to be loved. There are still Bibles to be printed and nations to be won over to our Lord Jesus. Heaven won't shut down because of Y2K.

I'm not saying that there won't be problems. It is very possible that a time of darkness is coming soon. When this will occur, I do not know. Nevertheless, there are still many dreams to be dreamed, and your vision still needs to be fulfilled. We each need to look beyond the year 2000 into a future that remains in the hand of our Father–one that involves each of our personal destinies. I believe Christ's coming is near–of that I am sure–but the gospel must still be preached in every nation, which has not yet been fulfilled.

The Lord is in the process of preparing His Bride. He wants each of us to discover our gifts and callings. He wants all of His children to find their place in His Body and to begin to fulfill that which He has called them to do.

We are in the greatest period of human history thus far. We must enter the next millennium equipped with one of the mightiest forces on this planet—our dreams. Dreams are very powerful weapons against the enemy's plans of despair. God always saves His best "wine" for last. This is the Church's finest hour. We are entering a time when men and women will begin to dream dreams once again.

"I Have a Dream"

Many people immediately recognize the statement, "I have a dream," and know who said it. The Lord wants us each to grab hold of these words for our lives. He wants us to have a dream. He wants us to have a vision or some kind of goal for our lives that we have received straight from His hand. We each need to believe that we have a destiny, a purpose the Lord desires to help us fulfill. This will help us through the most difficult times.

The most powerful weapon on earth is not a bomb dropped from the air or launched from an aircraft carrier. The most powerful weapon on earth is a vision dropped into the soul of a man by the Spirit of God and launched onto the earth by faith. Faith calls things that are not as though they were (see Rom. 4:17). This is why Jesus said:

> *...Have faith in God. For verily I say unto you, That whosoever shall say unto this mountain, Be thou removed, and be thou cast into the sea; and shall not doubt in his heart, but shall believe that those things which he saith shall come to pass; he shall have whatsoever he saith* (Mark 11:22-23).

Jesus also said, "to him that believes, all things are possible" (see Mk. 9:23). All God needs is a willing heart into which He can plant a little seed. With that seed He will plant a hope or a vision of how things could or should be. God gave Dr. Martin Luther King, Jr., a dream. Dr. King said in his famous speech in 1963 during the march on Washington, D.C. in front of the Lincoln Memorial, "I have a dream that one day every valley shall be exalted, every hill and mountain shall be made low, the rough places will be made plain, the crooked places made straight, and the glory of the Lord shall be revealed and all flesh shall see it together" (see Is. 40:4-5).

His dream was that someday all of God's children, regardless of race or culture or social upbringing, would be able to sing from every countryside, "Let Freedom Ring." Not only is Dr. King's dream already a reality in Heaven, but it is also beginning to be fulfilled on earth as men and women of God around the world have begun to come together as one family, the Body of Christ. This is God's true purpose and "the mystery" of all the ages.

> *That in the dispensation of the fulness of times He might gather together in one all things in Christ, both which are in heaven, and which are on earth; even in Him* (Ephesians 1:10).

As we saw in Chapter Eight, we need to learn and grow together. We need to see each other as brothers and sisters in the Lord, regardless of the color of our skin. Racial walls must come down. We must help one another see the beauty and diversity of our dreams and callings and make ourselves available to lend a hand to help our brothers and sisters fufill their dreams. After all, we have the same Father, and *we are our brother's keeper* (see Gen. 4:9-10).

The Dream Maker and the Dream Breaker

We all need encouragement from one another. God is the "dream maker," but we have an enemy who is a "dream breaker." Many of us grew up with the saying, "Sticks and stones may break my bones, but words can never hurt me." Well, that is not completely true. Words can and do hurt. The Bible states that life and death are in the power of the tongue (see Prov. 18:21).

There are many who have become discouraged and are living with broken dreams. Divorce, damaged relationships, unemployment, and sickness are just a few of the many ways in which dreams have become shattered on the rocks of despair.

Many of us heard words like these when we were growing up: "You can't do that." "You'll never amount to anything." "That is just not the way things are done." How sad. We all need encouragement from time to time. I needed encouragement to complete this book. Often we just need a little extra support to be able to pick ourselves up and begin again.

My friend John, whom I mentioned in the introduction, probably had no idea how much his dream about my writing encouraged me. There were many times when I just wanted to throw in the towel and give up; however, just knowing that my heavenly Father was "for me" encouraged me to keep on going (see Rom. 8:31). It is important to say that "word" to others and to share your dreams with them too. Who knows how much it will mean in their lives!

God believes in you, and He is in the business of mending broken dreams and of helping His children to begin again. He truly is the great encourager. He told Moses to not be afraid, because He would be with him. He told Joshua to be strong and very courageous as he crossed over into enemy territory to claim the "promised land." He called Gideon a "mighty man of valor." He said David was a man after His own heart. He called Abraham His friend.

The Lord knows that the enemy tries to discourage His people time and again:

> *So I returned, and considered all the oppressions that are done under the sun: and behold the tears of such as were oppressed, and they had no comforter; and on the side of their oppressors there was power; but they had no comforter* (Ecclesiastes 4:1).

By My Spirit

The Holy Spirit is the only One who can deliver you from the oppressive power of satan. It is through His anointing and His encouragement that many who were once weakened by satan's onslaughts can now stand up and fight for the faith. Always remember that the battle is the Lord's. Let Him fight it for you.

The Holy Spirit empowered and equipped our forefathers for the task of establishing and governing this nation. He strengthened and directed men of God like William Booth, William Seymour, John Wesley, Roger Williams, and Martin Luther. He set men and women such as Dwight Moody, Charles Finney, Smith Wigglesworth, Kathryn Kuhlman, and Maria Woodworth-Etter on fire for God. Today, He has placed a vision in thousands upon thousands of men and women to reach this generation with the gospel.

Let God birth a dream in you like He did in these men and women. Their great achievements were great because they were ordinary men and women with an extraordinary God.

The world tells us: "You can't do it." "It will never work." "It's too big to accomplish." "You're too old to embark now." "It will never fly." But God says, "Go for it! Try to do whatever I put in your heart." As the following quote, which I saw on the back of a shirt, says: "The dreams of a child become the destiny of a man."

The same discouraging words that the world says today were said to Christopher Columbus, who helped discover America; to the Wright brothers, who pioneered flight; and to Alexander Graham Bell, who helped invent the telephone. These statements were also made to Thomas Edison, who helped discover the light bulb; and even to Mother Theresa as she was heading off toward India to work among the poor and the lepers. These words have been said to every person who ever tried to do something for the good of mankind. Thank God that these men and women stood their ground against all the lies of the enemy and never gave up on their dreams.

The world still looks down on many of us in the Body of Christ. We still hear things like: "They'll never amount to much." "I knew that would happen." "It serves them right, you know. They certainly got what was coming to them." "I just knew he couldn't do it." "I told you so"...and on and on.

Anyone who tries to rise a little higher becomes the target of such criticism. Some people have said that the only books that sell are the ones written by famous authors or by people who have a recognized public platform. I was turned down on my first attempts to publish, but God believed in me and helped me to keep the dream alive. God can do things in any way He wants. I've never been to a Bible school or seminary, nor have I gone to writing school. Yet the Lord actually showed me this book in its completed form in a dream to encourage me to finish it. He also showed me it would lead many to recommit their lives to Him and to begin to fulfill His destiny for them.

God says in His Word that He chooses the foolish to confound the wise (see 1 Cor. 1:27). I simply had to decide to make up my mind to obey God and not man. Sometimes the pen can be mightier than the sword.

Prep School

Now, I'm not telling everyone to go out and write a book. There is a time of preparation that is needed before any strong anointing for ministry comes. I know I am not quite there yet, and more than likely, neither are you. I'm just doing my best to follow my dreams toward God's destiny for me.

Here are four words God gave me in a dream that are steps in preparation: *tested, tried, faithful,* and *durable.* God is taking many of us through a new type of schooling these days; it's called "prep school."

Dreams don't come to you only in your sleep at night. Your dream may come to you as an intense desire to accomplish something for God in your life. Remember, God gives us the desires of our hearts (see Ps. 37:4).

Even when dreams do come in the night, they won't come about overnight. What I mean to say is, the Lord will bring you through a very necessary preparation time. There is a price to pay. Salvation may come as a free gift, but sanctification takes a lot of time and hard work. Those who have fulfilled a dream can share with you what it took for them to succeed. Fulfilling their dreams wasn't easy.

The Holy Spirit takes us all into His "classroom," and as the Teacher, He sees and knows everything that goes on.

You can't get away with anything. There is no skipping class, and you'll have to take each test over and over again until you pass it. God requires this because He wants us to learn "whole life" lessons. So if you end up fulfilling your dream but start losing your family in the process, you will likely have to wait to make it to the next level.

God's desire is that you pass all His tests with an "A" and graduate to the next dream level, but He still wants you to hold on to those truths you started out with and to take them with you to the end. If you lose any along the way, you will have to start over again. Only as you keep the Lord first and your family second in your line of priorities will He allow you to be "enrolled" in His "dream school" again.

Dream School

In Chapter Four, I mentioned our trip to India. My wife and I went to India because of a dream Sue was given. Neither one of us had ever considered going to India before this, but after Sue's dream we knew that God wanted us to go.

In the dream, my wife found herself on a college campus. There she entered through two doors. When she turned around, she could hardly believe her eyes. She appeared to be in India. Her friend in the dream asked Sue if she thought that they were in India. She then asked my wife what she thought they should do. Sue told her friend to "*keep walking*."

After what seemed like a long tour of India, Sue saw two more doors. As she walked through them she found herself back outside on the college campus.

The Lord was clearly telling us that He was going to take us to school. Part of our classroom training was a trip to India. It is amazing how one dream could change the destiny of our lives. Because of one dream, there are now thousands of people in India, England, and Russia hearing about God's love for them.

Dreams are part of God's "School of the Spirit." They are one means through which God communicates His will and plan for our lives. Dreams propel us toward our destiny. Sometimes when we're not quite sure what to do, we are exhorted to *just keep walking.*

If you don't believe in dreams, God may have to visit someone who does. For you see, if you believe in dreams, you will follow them and bring them to pass. Then God can give you more. Each dream will take you on in God's "School of the Spirit." In this school, all things are possible. God's dreams become reality.

The Lord must prepare our hearts so that we can dream His dreams. Just like my wife had to have an operation in order to have more children, the Lord wants to "perform surgery" on our hearts so that He can birth His dreams in us again. His dreams go far beyond the limits of man. They are capable of causing the blind to see, the deaf to hear, and the lame to walk again.

We have to believe if we are to do the works of Jesus. The Lord is always wanting to take us higher. We have all learned many kinds of things in the natural. Now is the time for the supernatural power of God to become manifested through you and through me.

As I mentioned earlier, I dreamed of writing this book. I actually saw the book in its completed form. As it was being printed, I saw it coming out on a round turnstile, and I even saw people from other nations picking it up as it came off the press. I don't have many talents, but I love to write and I am a proficient sleeper. My wife has dreamed of playing the harp. Both of our dreams have taken a lot of work, but we have remained faithful and are now beginning to receive the fruit of seeing those dreams through to the end.

We know what a mess we are and have been, so we can earnestly encourage you. You also may feel like a mess right now, but rejoice. Remember, God chose little David to take down big Goliath. He also chose the cross, which looked like total defeat, to bring the greatest victory of all time. This was for your eternal salvation and for mine. Praise God if the world can't figure you out, for it couldn't figure out Christ either. Just start small and be patient. Soon you will see the Lord begin to add to your dream.

> *Better is the end of a thing than the beginning thereof: and the patient in spirit is better than the proud in spirit* (Ecclesiastes 7:8).

Dreams take much faith, patience, and hard work, but the outcome of a godly dream is worth all the difficulties you encounter along the way. Just like Sue's dream of India, the Lord can take you through a "door" and then bring you safely back again.

Dreams teach us to really trust the Lord and to not lean on our own understanding (see Prov. 3:5). As He gives you dreams He will teach you to yield fully to Him and to trust Him every step of the way. He wants you to rise up, throw off all manmade limitations, and go for it. Here is a word of encouragement you've probably heard a thousand times, but I'm going to give it to you anyway: "Don't give up!"

Some of you may be divorced and your dream is to remarry someday. Or maybe your dream is to see your relationship restored with your son or your daughter, or perhaps with a friend. Yet again, your dream may be to have a new job that will enable you to spend more time with your family. Or your dream may be to become an evangelist, a nurse, or a doctor. I just want to encourage you to keep going.

We each have Christ's promises that He will be with us, that He will never leave us or forsake us, and that He is greater than all the negative circumstances and disappointments that surround us. He reassures us that we can do anything through Him because He left us promises that we can stand firmly upon. You can fulfill your dreams because just like Moses, He is with you; just like Abraham, He is your Friend; and just like Joshua, you can be strong and very courageous.

Don't give up, and don't let satan talk you out of your dreams. He will steal them if you allow him to. Just don't listen to his lies. Hold on to your dreams and keep pressing forward. You are well able to take the land, so get radical about your dream. Dare to move ahead! Go for it with complete confidence because God is with you!

Look in the mirror in the morning and say to yourself these words of encouragement: "God believes in me. He says I can do it."

> *For I can do all things through Christ which strengtheneth me* (Philippians 4:13).

Here is an anonymous but inspiring poem entitled "Don't You Quit":

When things go wrong, as they sometimes will,
When the road you're trudging seems all up hill;
When the funds are low and the debts are high,
And you want to smile, but you have to sigh;
When care is pressing you down a bit,
Rest if you must, but *don't you quit*;

Life is queer with its twists and turns,
As every one of us sometimes learns;
And many a fellow turns about,
When he might have won if he'd stuck it out;
Don't give up though the pace seems slow,
You may succeed with another blow;
Often the goal is nearer than,
It seems to a faint and faltering man;
Often the struggler has given up,
When he might have captured the victor's cup;
And he learned too late when the night came down,
How close he was to the golden crown;
Success is failure turned upside down,
The silver tint of the clouds of doubt;
And you never can tell how close you are,
It may be near when it seems afar;
So stick to the fight when you're the hardest hit,
It's when things seem worst that *you must not quit.*"

* * *

Father, we come boldly to You in the name of Jesus. We ask You to inspire and empower us to dream once again. Birth in us Your dreams of being who and what You have called us to be. Help those of us who were told that we would never amount to anything to mount up with wings as eagles. Help us to soar to new heights and to climb every mountain on the way to our final destination. Help us to never give up on our dreams. Amen.

Chapter Twelve

Fulfilling the Dream

Dreams are necessary because they are what cause us to push onward in life. We can compare ourselves to the little engine in the children's story that said, "I think I can." After a while, he was saying, "I know I can." Seeing dreams fulfilled is one of the most exciting things in life. Unfortunately, many dreams are still lying dormant and must be revived and fulfilled.

Look at the life of Joseph. It didn't look like the dreams he was given as a young man would ever come to pass. Even his own family didn't understand. There will be those in your own family that may not understand either. However, despite many adversities, Joseph still held on to his integrity; and after his dream was fulfilled, he was able to bless his own family and even those who were his enemies.

Fulfilling the Dream

One of the associate pastors at our church, Mike Shepherd, once said: "Although we can do all things *through*

Christ, we can't do anything without Him." This is a good confession for each of us to make. God has always chosen the foolish to confound the wise (see 1 Cor. 1:27). He often uses "cracked pots" and "bent candles." He is not about to change His policy on this issue, because we are too prone to claiming glory for ourselves instead of giving credit to whom credit is due.

The truth is, we really are nothing without Him. Anyone who thinks I could have written even one page of this book on my own ability doesn't know me very well. This book is the fulfillment of a dream. We all need dreams. As it says in Proverbs 29:18:

> *Where there is no vision, the people perish: but he that keepeth the law, happy is he.*

The word *perish* can mean "to let go of the reigns." We all need some type of a vision to hold on to with both hands. God is the "dream maker." Because He is the One who can make our dreams come true we should never let go.

Dreams die every day. They go to the grave without having the opportunity to fulfill their potential. I want to encourage you to never give up on the dreams God has given you. On the other hand, if the Lord has never given you a dream or a strong desire in your heart to do something for Him, then get behind someone who already has a dream in motion. As you help others with their dreams, God will help you with yours.

My wife and I want to encourage people to follow their dreams, especially those people who think God could never use them. Neither Sue nor I believed in ourselves at first, but the Lord didn't give up on us; and He won't give up on you. Let us be like Mary, who said, "Be it unto me according to Thy word" (Lk. 1:38b). Let us follow the example of our Lord who said, "Lo, I come (in the volume of the book it is written of Me,) to do Thy will, O God" (Heb. 10:7). *I believe it is written of each of us to fulfill our dreams.*

The last portion of the word the Lord gave me in Chapter Ten said that God would "*retain things no longer.*" To retain something is to hold it back. There are enough evil plans in the world already. God wants to help you bring to pass some positives plans, for a change. To say it plainly, you can't retain God. You can't put Him in a box because He will break out of it. You can't kill Him because He will arise.

In the same manner, God is birthing dreams, and *they shall be born.* I think the Lord is saying, "Look! Open your eyes; there is nothing to hold you back. Go for it and do it now. Just do it!" You can't retain what God has ordained. Ask God what He would have you do. You may think that what you do for God doesn't make much of a difference, but it does. Always remember that God chooses Davids to take down Goliaths (see 1 Sam. 17) and donkeys to speak to prophets (see 2 Pet. 2:15-16).

The following story from an unknown author has been a great inspiration to me.

Make a Difference

While walking along a beach, a man saw someone in the distance leaning down, picking something up, and throwing it into the ocean. As he came closer, he saw thousands of starfish that the tide had thrown onto the beach. Unable to return to the ocean during low tide, the starfish were dying. He observed a young man picking up the starfish one by one and throwing them back into the water. After watching the seemingly futile effort, the observer said, "There must be thousands of starfish on this beach. *It would be impossible for you to get to all of them. There are simply too many. You can't possibly save enough of them to make any difference at all.*" The young man smiled as he continued to pick up another starfish and toss it back into the ocean. "*It made a difference to that one,*" he replied.

Insignificant Dreamers Making a Difference

Many of you who are reading this doubt that God can ever use you. You may think God only does what is big or spectacular and your dream is too small. Your dream may simply be to help a family member or another person whom the Lord has put on your heart to help. He may be asking you to pray with a person down the block who has just lost a loved one. Perhaps you can visit someone who is sick or is in prison. If you make a positive difference in even one person's life, God will make a positive difference in yours.

Those who seem to be insignificant now will be used as a sign in the latter days to show God's abundant mercy and grace. Your life can and does make a difference. If you feel insignificant or you have a problem with inferiority and low self-esteem, start praising God *now*. The Lord is going to raise up a whole new breed of insignificant people right out of the seas of humanity.

God can use the weak, the immature, and the insecure. Just like the bent candle in Chapter Five, rivers of living water can issue forth from below the surface, creating a flood that will flow out to the nations.

He may choose those of you who were former gang members to reach inner city gangs. Troubled teens who were once told they would never amount to much will be used to help other teens overcome the same limitations that our society has imposed upon them. Those who have been delivered from the homosexual lifestyle through the grace of Christ will be used to reach out to those who haven't even come out of the closet yet.

Those He has delivered from alcohol and drugs will be used to help others who are still trapped in these harmful addictions. He will take those of you who have had abortions to demonstrate His love and forgiveness to those who feel they have no one to turn to.

God will meet many of you at the crossroads of your life like He met me. He will give a new direction in life so that you can follow only Him. He will pick up many of you from the highway of life, brush you off, and clean you up. Then, with Him on the inside, you will see that you are "pure gold" and are precious and valuable to Him. He will give hope to those of you who feel hopeless. He will provide for your every need. He will give you His new hope to be a steady anchor for your soul.

You will "drink" from His fountain of living waters, and new tongues will flow from your lips, even praise unto our God (see Acts 2:11). You will sense His presence like never before, and you will rejoice with joy unspeakable and show forth His glory.

God is raising up mothers, fathers, children, grandparents, athletes, homemakers, artists, filmmakers, singers, writers, publishers, cartoonists, inventors, teachers, cooks, telephone operators, doctors, and, yes, even lawyers! Many in Hollywood are now returning to Him. He is raising up leaders from among those with blue collars, white collars, no collars, and even those with their collars on backward.

The Lord wants to raise up people from the youngest child to the oldest "youth." He is returning us to what made

America great–the dreams and hard work of many whose foundation is the Lord. Just find a place somewhere and make a start! Those who were afraid to speak, sing, or play before a handful of people will be used to reach thousands. As T.L. Osborn once said, "If it's good for God, good for you, and good for others, go for it. If God wants to close the door, trust me, He knows how."

Ask the Lord to stir up once again all the gifts He placed in you. Ask Him to restore every gift He has placed within His Body, the Church. God is working in us and through us to tell the world of His love for everyone everywhere. If God can use me, I'm sure He can use you. If He can use us, He can use everyone to bring glory to His name.

As we transformed ones build God's house, we will truly be changed. We will be the children who "*shall be born*" ***again*** and lift up glorious praise to our God. According to Psalm 102:18, this is the very purpose for which our generation was created. God is raising up a people who will "do exploits" for Him (see Dan. 11:32). They will be those who know their God and are known of Him. They will follow the Lamb wherever He goes. They will go God's way and not their own way. They will be men and women who are "fishers of men," taking the good news of Christ to all nations.

These men and women, boys and girls, may still look like "bent candles" on the outside, but on the inside they will sing a "new song." Together their light will shine like a lighthouse bringing all the lost ships safely to shore. These new creations are worth much more than gold to God. They will step out of their boats and move from fear to freedom as they come to experience true fellowship with the rest of God's family.

As young men and women of God who are part of His anointed generation, they will become all God meant for them to be. They will say no to drugs and will lay down their weapons in order to take up the two-edged sword of the Word in their hearts. They will refuse to give up on their dreams and will press on to fulfill God's plan for their lives. They will see God's ultimate dream come to pass and will shine in their Father's Kingdom forevermore.

These beloved of the Lord will have pure hearts and will be motivated by a holy zeal to build their Father's house. And they will not do it for reward or outward show, but will work from a thankful heart of love that says, "Thank You, God, for having delivered me from this present evil world and for transferring me into the Kingdom of Your dear Son" (see Col. 1:13).

Happily Ever After

> *For we are His workmanship, created in Christ Jesus unto good works, which God hath before ordained that we should walk in them* (Ephesians 2:10).

The word *workmanship* in this verse is the Greek word *poema.* We are God's "poem," His work of art. You and I are God's dream. He desires to have us in Heaven with Him for all eternity so that He can shower us with His love and grace and show us what a great Father He really is. Only your sin will keep you out of His Heaven, and only Christ's blood has the cleansing power to make you white as snow.

God's ultimate dream will be fulfilled when His born-again sons and daughters from every family and people under the sun will be sitting around His table. Jew and Gentile, light or dark-colored skin—it makes no difference to Him. His heart will be truly glad when He can look into the precious faces of His whole family gathered around Him.

God longs to teach each and every one of us about His love, grace, and mercy. He wants us to enjoy all of His creation throughout eternity. The Lord has allotted a time period for this unveiling and He calls it "eternity."

May we be those who will make an impact on our neighborhood, city, country, and world. Don't despise the day of small things. Every river started as a trickle. Let your lights shine as those who are waiting with anticipation for their Master's return. Keep your vessel full, and watch and pray, for your redemption draws near (see Lk. 21:28,36). Jesus is coming soon! He loves you and is coming for His Bride.

Let's work together, hand-in-hand, joyfully building our Father's house. Let's share the "good news" with those He has placed in our lives. Let's turn around, honk our horns, and drive up on some lawns to tell the owners about our precious Savior. Let's talk about His wonderful love, grace, and mercy, which He has so freely bestowed upon us with those He has placed before us. Let's fall in love with our God once again and let others know that He alone is worthy of receiving our all. "*Let the redeemed of the Lord say so*" (Ps. 107:2a)!

Don't give up on your dreams; keep pressing in. He who is faithful will keep that which He has committed unto you against that day (see 2 Tim 1:12). *The effect of every vision shall be retained no longer.* The fulfillment of God's dream will one day be a reality. The impact of your life will soon be unleashed upon your world. This will be your finest hour. God has saved you for last!

The end...
...or is it just the beginning?

* * *

Lord Jesus, according to Your Word, I believe that all kinds of things are getting ready to take place, and I pray that You would allow me to be a part of what You are doing in the earth today. I ask You with all my heart that I may be one of those who will rise up to become an even greater witness of Your love and power. Please guide me daily by the Holy Spirit and help me to understand more fully that it is all by Your grace. Please help me step-by-step in my relationship with You. I want to know You, Lord, above all else in my life. I pray that You will keep my family close to You and will help me see Your beauty in my brothers and sisters regardless of their color, culture, or denominational affiliation. Teach me to once again follow Your dreams for my life that I may fulfill Your purpose. Help me to keep my eyes open and my heart pure. I love You, Jesus, and look forward to the day when I will behold You in all Your glory. Thank You for drawing all men to You as we lift You up and glorify Your name. Amen.

Appendix

Thoughts From the Author's Heart Regarding Accountability, Testing, and the Interpreting of Dreams

Honesty and integrity are vital in the area of dreams and visions. I have tried to be honest about my dreams and visions, as well as to openly share with you some of my personal struggles. I can say with a certainty that my intentions are pure for wanting to glorify my Lord and Savior and not to bury the gifts, words, and dreams He has given me. My heart regarding this book can best be described with the words from one of King David's psalms:

> *I have told everyone the Good News that You forgive men's sins. I have not been timid about it, as You well know, O Lord. I have not kept this Good News hidden in my heart, but have proclaimed Your lovingkindness and truth to all the congregation* (Psalm 40:9-10 TLB).

Dare to Believe

The Scriptures clearly teach that those who continually lie, in contrast to an honest heart, will be cast into a lake of fire in the end of time (see Rev. 21:8). I have included this section only to affirm that I've tried to do my best, through the integrity of my heart, to share what the Lord has given me. I have re-read what I have written and feel confident that I am presenting an accurate and honest work.

I know I will answer to God in regard to what I have written in this book. I know that some may judge me because they still do not believe that God works this way. I must take into account what I have already written in Chapter Three–that some people want to remain where they are and others choose to walk in their own ways.

Also, there will be others, such as I wrote about in Chapter Four, who may be walking with us but are still unable to see the "harvest of fish" that is taking place all around us. Many are blind to the Son, who is shining His light upon them from above.

Understanding the World of Dreams

This whole experience with the world of dreams has been quite a time of learning and growth for me. Even though I've made many mistakes along the way, I wouldn't trade this walk with the Holy Spirit for anything. There have been many struggles and difficulties along the way, but the Lord has been faithful to "hold my hand" through it all. I would like to exhort anyone who feels the Lord is starting to deal with them in this area to be very careful to use the utmost integrity in these matters.

I want to exhort everyone who believes that the Lord is starting to speak to them in dreams or visions to begin by writing them down. Be aware of the "tyranny of the urgent." Write down your dreams, then put them aside and wait for the Lord's leading. Most dreams will be for you only; they are not to be shared with anyone except those whom you trust and who trust you. Make sure you really study your Bible, for if your dream comes from God, then the principle of the dream or vision will always be found in His Word. As Isaiah 8:20 says, "...if they speak not according to this word, it is because there is no light in them."

Dreams of destiny usually come with a very strong anointing, are very clear, and are easy to remember. The Lord usually wakes me up immediately after a dream that will have a major significance in my life. Most of the dreams you receive will not be as clear as a dream of destiny. Many times these lesser dreams are given just to help you in your journey. These dreams deal with character flaws and the little areas of your life that the Lord is still dealing with you about.

If you have a dream that is blurred or is unclear in its meaning, don't worry about it. If it is important for your life, the Holy Spirit will give it to you again. A friend of mine was given the exact same dream three times in one night. Also, don't make major decisions because of a dream until you have prayed about it and know God's will. As you grow in this area, the Holy Spirit will work with you and will teach you how to tell which dreams come from Him and which come from your flesh or from the world.

Because of some dreams I have been given, entire sections of Scriptures opened up to me that were not at all clear to me before. There are hundreds of verses in the Bible that are now a significant part of me as a result of searching the Word after waking up from a dream.

Also, there are people who previously never had the Lord speak to them in dreams, but who started to have dreams and visions imparted to them almost immediately after reading portions of this manuscript. These things will continue as we approach Jesus' second coming. This is why I am including some precautions, as well as some help with interpretation.

Be Aware

The Word of God is our final authority. It alone contains the light that shines in the darkness. If anyone fails to affirm and follow this principle, beware! Also, take heed as to whom you share these things with. I was so excited the first time I received a word from the Lord that I thought I was supposed to share it with everyone. This is what Joseph did with his brothers, and it led to disastrous results for him. So be careful. You don't want to end up in any pits like he did.

Be patient! The Lord knows what He is doing. Remember, if the Lord gives you something, He will help you know what to do with it. Ask Him to help you and then wait patiently for Him to open the doors. He'll give you direction and insight as to what to do.

The Bible clearly teaches that there will be those who produce false revelations as well:

> *So why are you trying to find out the future by consulting witches and mediums? Don't listen to their whisperings and mutterings. Can the living find out the future from the dead? Why not ask your God?* (Isaiah 8:19 TLB)

Second Timothy 4:1 says that in the last days many will depart from the faith and begin to heed seducing spirits and doctrines of devils. The Lord has made it clear how He speaks to His people: He speaks through His Word, the Bible. Any dream or vision contrary to the Word of God must be rejected. God clearly says He will speak through prophetic utterances and dreams in these last days. However, He has made it just as clear that to seek any knowledge outside of what He has approved in His Word will lead only to deception.

Make sure you stay away from horoscopes, psychics, and fortune-tellers because according to Deuteronomy 18:9-14, their practices are an abomination to God. Saul sought the witch of Endor because he did not want to wait for God to give him an answer. This sin caused not only the deaths of his sons, but it cost him his own life as well. You can't afford to take God's clear instructions about this lightly.

As I said before, honesty and integrity are very important, and we must give an account to Him for the knowledge we possess, as well as what we pass on to others. There are many humorous incidents I could share with you with regard to this area of my life. I think the Lord is beginning to trust me with more revelations and is recognizing that I have learned from my own mistakes.

Don't just follow a dream. The Lord will usually confirm His will in other ways. Often it will be through other people speaking into your life. God still usually uses two or three witnesses to establish every word.

Here is another word of warning: *Many dreams come out of an active imagination.* Some could even be inspired by satan. If you're caught up in the world's ways and have never given the Lord full control over your life, then I would be very cautious in this area. God's dreams always point you to God's words.

Not every dream has meaning for your life. With me, the Holy Spirit anoints certain dreams and makes them so clear to me that I couldn't forget them if I tried to. But just because you have a very clear dream and you can remember it well doesn't necessarily mean that it is a God-given dream. Don't allow your mind to be filled with foolishness from a lot of television or other media. I doubt the Lord will even begin to speak to you in this area unless you surrender these things to Him.

> *Who may climb the mountain of the Lord and enter where He lives? Who may stand before the Lord?* ***Only those with pure hands and hearts, who do not practice dishonesty and lying.*** *They will receive God's own goodness as their blessing from Him, planted in their lives by God Himself, their Savior* (Psalm 24:3-5 TLB).

Spend quality time in God's Word if you really have a desire for God to speak to you in dreams. This will greatly enhance your prayer time and cause your faith to grow. The Lord will purify your heart as you spend that time with Him. I've noticed many times that after quality time with the Lord in prayer, my spirit becomes more open to receive revelation from the Holy Spirit. Often, it has been after times in His refreshing presence that He has spoken to me most clearly in dreams.

Testing Dreams

It is very important to be able to test a dream to see if it comes from God and to be able to interpret its meaning. God is in the business of edifying, exhorting, and comforting us. He is not into tearing us down. There are other Christian books available that can help you continue to grow and gain understanding in this area. I have included my own personal list of how you can test a dream to determine whether it is from God or not.

There are eight basic questions I ask myself, and recommend that you ask yourself concerning the source of a dream:

1. Does the dream seem to contradict God's overall nature of being a good and loving Father who desires the best for His children?

2. Does the dream contradict the written Word of God?

3. Does the dream glorify Christ and point people to the cross as the only way of salvation?

4. Does the dream build me (or someone else) up and cause me (or the other person) to desire an even closer walk with the Lord?

5. Is the dream producing fear in my life that is hindering me from moving with God, or does it promote the freedom I have in Christ?

6. Does the dream encourage me to get my answers from a certain person or from the world, or does the dream point me to Christ?

7. Does the dream seem to line up with God's overall plan for my life regarding things about which He has already spoken to me?

8. Does the dream encourage the fulfillment of the "great commission" to go into all the world and preach the gospel of Christ?

I have given you this list simply because there are many people in the world who have built a science out of interpreting dreams. However, many of their interpretations can be very misleading and deceptive and can lead a person into bondage.

Interpreting Dreams

Interpreting dreams is a major topic. I will give you just a few basic principles I have learned regarding how to interpret dreams. In Chapter One, I interpreted the image of my parents' house as meaning God's house. I did this simply because in my dream, the inside of my Father's house became the inside of a church.

God used this image because He knew how much I loved and respected my earthly father. Even though my father and I didn't always see eye to eye or entirely understand one another, I always held him in very high regard, similarly to how I would honor the Lord. However, I know that many people may not feel the same respect for their parents, and the house they grew up in may mean something completely different in their dreams.

Here are a few examples I have noticed that seem quite consistent: (I'm sure there are many more. I will only share what I've learned from my own dreams). *Old houses* usually represent that you are living in the past and the Lord wants to take you into the present.

The place your dream occurs can also be significant. You may want to observe whether your dream takes place in the front yard or the backyard, or in the inside or the outside of the house. The *front yard* usually represents the present and the *backyard*, the past. The *inside* of your house usually represents God working on your character, and the *outside* often relates to your outward image or public ministry.

Driveways, parking lots, and *garages* usually reveal that you are in a place of transition or a set waiting period. *Cars* can sometimes represent people, but they can also represent an automobile. How fast a vehicle is going is important too. Do the brakes work? What is the condition of the car? Do you need to slow down or speed up?

Water usually represents the outpouring of the Holy Spirit, but it can also represent actual flooding, peoples, and nations. Where the water is located and how clean or dirty it is can also be very important. Are you seeing yourself in a stream, a river, or out at sea? All of these can be important factors regarding the dream's interpretation.

The Lord will take you into the "School of the Spirit" to teach you these things, so don't be surprised if you find yourself in some *classroom* or in one of your previous jobs in your dream. If you are an adult and you find yourself in an elementary school, it probably means you are a bit behind in your training. The Lord just recently put me back in a high school classroom and told me I had three more years to go before I would even enter the ministry He has called me to.

Birds can be good or evil depending on the type of bird represented. For instance, I had a dream where a black bird with an unusual red mark on its head kept attacking me. I believe this bird may have represented satan or an evil spirit. A friend of mine had a dream in which she saw a black bird sitting on the arm of someone we both knew. I interpreted this to mean "depression or oppression." In the movie *It's a Wonderful Life*, Brother Billy had a black bird sitting on his arm and shoulder after Mr. Potter stole all his money. In dreams, I have also seen smaller black birds whispering false information in people's ears instructing them in the ways of false religions.

A white bird usually represents the Holy Spirit, as in my dream mentioned in Chapter Three. However, it could also represent other things, such as when Noah sent one out of the ark. Eagles usually represent the prophetic gifts or gifts of wisdom. My wife and I have both seen multi-colored birds in dreams. I actually saw one of these birds come down right over my head. I believe this represents the multiple anointings given by the Holy Spirit.

Snakes usually represent sin and evil and the one behind it. Most people can't identify what kind of snakes they see in their dreams. Since I used to study different kinds of snakes, the Lord shows me what type of snake to more accurately reveal the nature of the situation and the degree of danger involved. The size of the snake can be important as well.

Colors are also very significant. Red usually represents the blood of Christ, but it can also be a warning to stop or of impending danger. Blue usually represents the anointing of the Holy Spirit, but it can mean other things, depending on how it is used. Yellow and gold usually represent the glory of God upon a person or an object. White usually represents purity and holiness. Purple usually represents royalty. Many have seen Christ in a vision or dream wearing some type of purple clothing.

I share these few examples with you because these are the things I am most familiar with and have experienced myself. The Lord will usually speak to you using the knowledge of people, places, and circumstances that you understand. Many things in dreams represent themselves. Don't look for hidden meanings if the dream is already clear.

In Numbers 12:8, God says that He will speak to man in "dark speeches." The Bible says "we see through a glass, darkly" (1 Cor. 13:12). The Lord does this so that we will learn to put our faith and trust in Him. This is why He sometimes speaks to us in "riddles" in a dream. He is teaching us to seek after Him and to get to know Him even more.

One thing I would like to stress is that dream interpretations can vary greatly because of our differing backgrounds. However, because the Lord knows when every sparrow falls, He knows us each intimately, and to the point that He has every hair on our head numbered (see Mt. 10:29-30), there are certain things He will reveal to each of us that only we can interpret.

I've noticed that the more dreams I received, the easier it became to interpret them because the Lord began to use certain patterns with me. For example, He would sometimes give me more than one dream about a certain person before I realized that He wanted me to share the dream with him or her. One time He kept giving me a different dream night after night about the same person until I finally shared it with that person. As soon as I shared it, the dreams stopped. This was His merciful and patient way of revealing His will to me with regard to that dream.

At times, the Lord will also give those who know me a dream that is a riddle they cannot interpret on their own. He did this with Nebuchadnezzar–the Lord wouldn't reveal the interpretation of Nebuchadnezzar's dream to anyone but Daniel. The only way to be sure of the dream is to seek God in prayer and ask Him to reveal the interpretation or to show you who you should go to for counsel. Some dreams seem to have more than one interpretation. If you're not sure which interpretation is correct, then it might be better to discard it. Remember, if it is not clear enough or you forget it, then it probably wasn't important enough to begin with.

Daniel 1:17 says that God gave to Daniel and his three friends "knowledge and skill in all learning and wisdom," and to Daniel, "understanding of all visions and dreams." He can also do this for you and for me. Only the Holy Spirit can accurately interpret dreams because He is the One who gives them. I'll affirm the words of Daniel in this matter: "But there is a God in heaven that revealeth secrets, and maketh known...what shall be in the latter days..." (Dan. 2:28).

There is always a reason why God gives someone a dream or vision. Many times it is to give the individual knowledge in order that he or she can pray about an event so that it will not happen. Many people have shared how they were just minding their own business when suddenly they were given a vision in which someone they knew was in danger. This has happened to me as well.

One time while I was sitting on my couch, I was given a vision of a car going off the road. I knew immediately I was to pray for those people in the car so that not one would perish. After a short time of intercession, I felt a release in my spirit that everything would be all right. The fact that the Lord gives us a dream as a warning implies that the situation can be changed through prayer. If you're not sure what to do in a situation, always be sure to pray.

Watch for Pride

Our dreams and visions from God must never be taken beyond God's intention for giving them. Otherwise, there could be devastating results in our lives or the lives of those around us. The things that proceed from the Holy Spirit will always glorify the Lord alone and cause us to have more humility, rather than to fill us with pride.

Also, don't think there is something wrong with you if you've never received a dream or a vision. You may not have thought that much about them before. Some people claim that they don't dream at all. God can speak to you in many other ways, so don't condemn yourself if you've never been given a dream or if you can't remember them. You may ask God to make you more open to hearing from Him in this way and in other ways. However, your emphasis should be on receiving God's word for you and not on the particular vehicle He uses to deliver it.

If all you get from this book is just the desire to dream, then you've missed the whole point. *Our focus needs to be on Jesus and our relationship with Him.* We need to keep Him first whether we are given a dream or not. My desire is that each dream or word in this book will compel you toward a greater intimacy in your relationship with Christ. We need to learn to enter into His rest. We should not just seek to have dreams, but we should seek to know the One who gives them. We should seek to glorify Him alone and to find what is our part in His Body so that we all may work properly together to fulfill the "Great Commission."

Take heed when you think you are standing, lest you fall (see 1 Cor. 10:12). Pride goes before a fall (see Prov. 16:18). Satan is not stupid, so never underestimate him. He has had over 6,000 years on this planet to learn every trick available, so don't try to stand on your own. Put on the whole armor of God (see Eph. 6:13-18).

Paul received an abundance of revelation and was even caught up into the third Heaven according to Second Corinthians 12:1-4. Remember also, that an "evil messenger" was sent to buffet or hinder him (see 2 Cor. 12:7-10). I'm sure that we all have had our share of troubles from this menacing source. Satan desires to take us down, but through God's grace we have already obtained the victory.

Let the Lord be your strength. His grace alone is sufficient. He has made provision for victory in your life as well:

> *Put on all of God's armor so that you will be able to stand safe against all strategies and tricks of Satan. For we are not fighting against people made of flesh and blood, but against persons without bodies–the evil rulers of the unseen world, those mighty satanic beings and great evil princes of darkness who rule this world; and against huge numbers of wicked spirits in the spirit world* (Ephesians 6:11-12 TLB).

Now the Lord in us is greater than all the evil in the world, and we are not the greater, but the lesser. If we decrease, His power will increase in our lives.

Prayer of Increase

> *Call unto Me, and I will answer thee, and show thee great and mighty things, which thou knowest not* (Jeremiah 33:3).

Finally, I want to pray for all those who love the Lord and want His help in fulfilling their dreams. I don't claim to have arrived, nor do I understand why God has allowed me the privilege of writing this book. Yet I assure you that what is contained in these pages didn't come just from me. The Scriptures say that we have not because we ask not (see Jas. 4:2), so we will now ask God to increase the anointing of His Holy Spirit in your life:

* * *

Father, I come boldly before You as Your child in the name of Your most precious Son, Jesus. I ask You now to increase Your dreams and visions to all who have read this book. Give us the wisdom to know who to share Your dreams with and who not to.

Open our spiritual eyes to understand Your heart toward Your people, especially Israel, Your chosen people. Cause us not to do things by ourselves, but to consult and work with our brothers and sisters.

Teach us how to enter into new realms in the Spirit and bring us to Your Holy mountain so that we can share Your heart with those who are still in the valleys. Give us Your heart to reach out to those who are lost so that they may find their way back home to Your house and receive healing.

Lord, I ask that You will anoint, clothe, empower, and change all those who have prayed this prayer. Let them rise up in the strength of Your Spirit. Lord, I pray that no person who picks up this book will miss out on Heaven, but may each and every one call upon Your name and be saved. May we hear Your voice, our Abba, Father.

Help us to find and fulfill the purpose for which we were born. Give us Your dreams in the early morning hours, while it is still day, and give us Your songs in the night. Let them bring light, hope, and revelation to Your Church and to those who don't know You yet.

Give us dreams of our destiny so that we may serve You all the days of our lives. Let them cause us to desire to rebuild Your house, and help us to spread Your "good news" across the earth. Jesus, we praise You, adore You, and anticipate with great joy, Your soon return. Even now, come Lord Jesus! Hallelujah! Amen.

* * *

Say not ye, There are yet four months, and then cometh harvest? behold, I say unto you, Lift up your eyes, and look on the fields; for they are white already to harvest (John 4:35).

If you live in the St. Louis or Illinois area and would like to be part of a home group, please contact:

Life Christian Center
13301 Gravois Road
St. Louis, MO 63127
314-843-5575

If you are from another country but live in St. Louis, and would like to find out about or support an international fellowship, or take an "English as a Second Language" class, contact:

Bansi Brahmbhatt
6922 Lansdown
St. Louis, Missouri 63109
314-645-9977
savethelost@hotmail.com

If you are from another country but live in the U.S. and would like to take part in a world evangelism class contact:

U.S. Center for World Missions/Gateway Office
Ken Shirkey
201 S. Skinker Blvd.
St. Louis, MO 60105
314-863-5503
Fax: 314-721-1092
ks4gateway@aol.com

If you desire to take part or help with David Taylor's ministry, please contact:

Resurrection Media Ministries
P.O. Box B
St. Louis, MO 63121

We are collecting dreams from around the world that we believe the Lord is giving as He speaks to His Church today. If you have received a vision or a dream that you feel the Lord has given to you, we would like to extend an invitation to you to share it with us by mail.

We will not be able to return your dream, and there will be no payment for them; however, we believe that if the Lord puts it in our heart to use them, they will greatly benefit the Body of Christ. Your dream or vision could be a significant instrument in reaching the lost with the gospel, and this is our ultimate aim. May God bless you as you continue to seek His will in your life. Please contact us at the following address:

Bart and Sue Druckenmiller
P.O. Box 153
St. Louis, MO 63088

6:1

Other *Destiny Image titles* you will enjoy reading

DREAM INTERPRETATION

by Herman Riffel.

Many believers read the scriptural accounts of dreams and never think it could happen to them. Today, though, many are realizing that God has never ceased using dreams and visions to guide, instruct, and warn. This book will give you a biblical understanding of dreams that you never had before!

ISBN 1-56043-122-9

UNDERSTANDING THE DREAMS YOU DREAM

by Ira Milligan.

Have you ever had a dream in which you think God was speaking to you? Here is a practical guide, from the Christian perspective, for understanding the symbolic language of dreams. Deliberately written without technical jargon, this book can be easily understood and used by everyone. Includes a complete dictionary of symbols.

ISBN 1-56043-284-5

DREAMS: GIANTS AND GENIUSES IN THE MAKING

by Herman Riffel.

Did you know that great scientific discoveries were made through dreams? Many kings and leaders dreamed of their conquests, and famous musical pieces were composed through dreams. Learn how you too—like Einstein, Alexander the Great, and Mozart—can become a giant and a genius by following your dreams!

ISBN 1-56043-171-7

DREAMS: WISDOM WITHIN

by Herman Riffel.

This foremost full-gospel authority discusses how and why God uses dreams. He shows how incorrect assumptions about dreams have caused us to ignore this essential way in which God speaks to His people.

ISBN 1-56043-007-9

Available at your local Christian bookstore.

Internet: http://www.reapernet.com

6:28